rary

The
Korean War

Titles in the World History Series

The Age of Augustus
The Age of Exploration
The Age of Feudalism
The Age of Napoleon
The Alamo
America in the 1960s
The American Revolution
Ancient Chinese Dynasties
Ancient Greece
The Ancient Near East
Architecture
The Assyrian Empire
Aztec Civilization
The Battle of the
    Little Bighorn
The Black Death
The Bombing of Pearl Harbor
The Byzantine Empire
Caesar's Conquest of Gaul
The California Gold Rush
The Chinese Cultural
    Revolution
The Civil Rights Movement
The Collapse of the
    Roman Republic
Colonial America
The Conquest of Mexico
The Constitution and the Founding of
    America
The Creation of Israel
The Crimean War
The Crusades
The Cuban Missile Crisis
The Decline and Fall of the Roman
    Empire
The Early Middle Ages
Egypt of the Pharaohs
Elizabethan England
The Enlightenment
The French Revolution
Greek and Roman
    Mythology
Greek and Roman Science

Greek and Roman Sport
Greek and Roman Theater
The History of Rock & Roll
The History of Slavery
Hitler's Reich
The Incan Empire
The Industrial Revolution
The Inquisition
The Italian Renaissance
The Korean War
The Late Middle Ages
The Louisiana Purchase
The Making of the Atom Bomb
The Mexican-American War
The Mexican Revolution
The Mexican War of
    Independence
Modern Japan
The Mongol Empire
The Persian Empire
Pirates
Prohibition
The Punic Wars
The Reagan Years
The Reformation
The Renaissance
The Rise and Fall of the
    Soviet Union
The Rise of Christianity
The Roaring Twenties
Roosevelt and the
    New Deal
Russia of the Tsars
The Salem Witch Trials
The Stone Age
The Titanic
Traditional Africa
Twentieth Century Science
Victorian England
The War of 1812
Westward Expansion
Women of Ancient Greece

WORLD
HISTORY SERIES

The
Korean War

by
Michael V. Uschan

Lucent Books, P.O. Box 289011, San Diego, CA 92198-9011

To Dick Herman, whose own personal history is as interesting, in its own way, as that of the Korean War.

Library of Congress Cataloging-in-Publication Data

Uschan, Michael V., 1942–
  Korean war / by Michael V. Uschan.
      p. cm.—(World history series)
Includes bibliographical references and index.
Summary: Discusses the history of a war without a winner, the beginning of the Cold War, the Cold War turns hot in Korea, North Korea suprises the world, victory at Inchon, China enters the war, the Korean War divides America, waging peace to win a war, and aftermath.
  ISBN 1-56006-704-7 /–02   √95/.9042
  1. Korean war, 1950–1953. I. Title. II. Series
  DS918.U578 2001
  951.904'2—dc21

                                        00-011527

Contents

Foreword

Each year on the first day of school, nearly every history teacher faces the task of explaining why his or her students should study history. One logical answer to this question is that exploring what happened in our past explains how the things we often take for granted—our customs, ideas, and institutions—came to be. As statesman and historian Winston Churchill put it, "Every nation or group of nations has its own tale to tell. Knowledge of the trials and struggles is necessary to all who would comprehend the problems, perils, challenges, and opportunities which confront us today." Thus, a study of history puts modern ideas and institutions in perspective. For example, though the founders of the United States were talented and creative thinkers, they clearly did not invent the concept of democracy. Instead, they adapted some democratic ideas that had originated in ancient Greece and with which the Romans, the British, and others had experimented. An exploration of these cultures, then, reveals their very real connection to us through institutions that continue to shape our daily lives.

Another reason often given for studying history is the idea that lessons exist in the past from which contemporary societies can benefit and learn. This idea, although controversial, has always been an intriguing one for historians. Those who agree that society can benefit from the past often quote philosopher George Santayana's famous statement, "Those who cannot remember the past are condemned to repeat it." Historians who subscribe to Santayana's philosophy believe that, for example, studying the events that led up to the major world wars or other significant historical events would allow society to chart a different and more favorable course in the future.

Just as difficult as convincing students to realize the importance of studying history is the search for useful and interesting supplementary materials that present historical events in a context that can be easily understood. The volumes in Lucent Books' World History Series attempt to present a broad, balanced, and penetrating view of the march of history. Ancient Egypt's important wars and rulers, for example, are presented against the rich and colorful backdrop of Egyptian religious, social, and cultural developments. The series engages the reader by enhancing historical events with these cultural contexts. For example, in *Ancient Greece*, the text covers the role of women in that society. Slavery is discussed in *The Roman Empire*, as well as how slaves earned their freedom. The numerous and varied aspects of everyday life in these and other societies are explored in each volume of the series. Additionally, the series covers the major political, cultural, and philosophical ideas as the torch of civilization is passed from ancient Mesopotamia and Egypt, through Greece, Rome, Medieval Europe, and other world cultures, to the modern day.

The material in the series is formatted in a thorough, precise, and organized manner. Each volume offers the reader a comprehensive and clearly written overview of an important historical event or period. The topic under discussion is placed in a broad, historical context. For example, *The Italian Renaissance* begins with a discussion of the High Middle Ages and the loss of central control that allowed certain Italian cities to develop artistically. The book ends by looking forward to the Reformation and interpreting the societal changes that grew out of the Renaissance. Thus, students are not only involved in an historical era, but also enveloped by the events leading up to that era and the events following it.

One important and unique feature in the World History Series is the primary and secondary source quotations that richly supplement each volume. These quotes are useful in a number of ways. First, they allow students access to sources they would not normally be exposed to because of the difficulty and obscurity of the original source. The quotations range from interesting anecdotes to farsighted cultural perspectives and are drawn from historical witnesses both past and present. Second, the quotes demonstrate how and where historians themselves derive their information on the past as they strive to reach a consensus on historical events. Lastly, all of the quotes are footnoted, familiarizing students with the citation process and allowing them to verify quotes and/or look up the original source if the quote piques their interest.

Finally, the books in the World History Series provide a detailed launching point for further research. Each book contains a bibliography specifically geared toward student research. A second, annotated bibliography introduces students to all the sources the author consulted when compiling the book. A chronology of important dates gives students an overview, at a glance, of the topic covered. Where applicable, a glossary of terms is included.

In short, the series is designed not only to acquaint readers with the basics of history, but also to make them aware that their lives are a part of an ongoing human saga. Perhaps they will then come to the same realization as famed historian Arnold Toynbee. In his monumental work, *A Study of History*, he wrote about becoming aware of history flowing through him in a mighty current, and of his own life "welling like a wave in the flow of this vast tide."

Important Dates in the History of the Korean War

1948
August 15, Republic of Korea (South Korea) formed in Seoul and Syngman Rhee elected president; United States turns over power to South Korea's new government.

1948
September 9, Democratic People's Republic of Korea (North Korea) formed in Pyongyang and Kim Il Sung is proclaimed premier.

1910
Japan annexes Korea.

June 25,
North Korea invades South Korea to begin the Korean War.

June 30,
President Truman orders U.S. ground forces into South Korea and a naval blockade of the Korean coast and authorizes the U.S. Air Force to begin bombing raids over North Korea.

August 1,
Retreating South Korean and U.S. troops establish the Pusan Perimeter.

October 1,
UN troops cross the 38th parallel into North Korea.

October 2,
China decides to enter the war.

October 14,
Chinese troops cross the Yalu River and enter North Korea.

October 15,
President Harry Truman and Gen. Douglas MacArthur meet on Wake Island.

October 19,
UN forces capture Pyongyang, North Korea's capital.

October 26,
Chinese army attacks UN forces fifty miles south of the Yalu River in the first battle between the two sides.

| 1910 | 1945 | 1950 | June | July | Aug, | Sept. | Oct. | Nov. |

1945
August 11, Korea is divided into Soviet and U.S. zones of occupation along the 38th parallel.

1949
September 29, President Harry S. Truman announces that the Soviet Union has exploded an atomic bomb.

1949
October 1, Mao Tse-tung proclaims the People's Republic of China.

July 5,
U.S. troops engage North Korean troops for the first time at a spot north of Osan, then retreat with heavy casualties.

September 19 to 29,
UN troops battle North Koreans and capture Seoul.

September 27,
General MacArthur gains permission to cross the 38th parallel into North Korea.

September 15,
U.S., British, Australian, New Zealand, Canadian, and Netherlands troops come ashore behind North Korean lines and capture Inchon; soldiers from the Pusan Perimeter push north to join them.

November 7 to December 9,
In the east, U.S. Marines encircled at Chosin Reservoir fight their way out after being surrounded by the Chinese. In the west, the U.S Army's Second and Twenty-fifth Divisions are battered.

December,
UN forces are driven back. Communist troops launch a major offensive, recross the 38th parallel, and begin a second invasion of South Korea.

December 23,
Gen. Walton H. Walker is killed when his jeep is struck by a truck. Gen. Matthew B. Ridgway takes command of the Eighth Army.

December 30,
U.S. Air Force planes near Yalu River encounter Red Chinese MiG-15 jet fighters in the first battle ever between jet planes.

June 13,
After a series of offensives and counteroffensives, both sides dig in and the front begins to stabilize near the 38th parallel.

May,
Peace talks deadlock over the issue of prisoners of war (POWs).

November 1,
The United States explodes the first hydrogen bomb, at Eniwetok Atoll in the Pacific.

June 23,
Soviet delegate Jacob Malik proposes truce talks.

July 10,
Peace talks begin at Kaesong.

June to October,
Stalemate along battlefront while truce talks remain stalled on the POW exchange issue.

December 5–8,
President-elect Dwight D. Eisenhower visits South Korea in order to fulfill his campaign promise.

| Dec. | 1951 | Jan. | Mar. | April | June | July | 1952 | 1953 | 2000 |

January 5,
Communist forces recapture Seoul.

March 1,
A UN counteroffensive begins and the UN line angles between the 37th and 38th parallels.

March 18,
Seoul is retaken by UN forces.

April 11,
President Truman recalls Gen. Douglas MacArthur and replaces him with General Ridgway; on April 19, MacArthur appears before Congress in hearings on his removal.

March 5,
Joseph Stalin dies; new Soviet premier Georgi Malenkov speaks of peaceful coexistence with the United States, giving new impetus to the stalled peace talks.

April 26,
Truce talks resume at Panmunjom.

July 27,
Cease-fire signed by Lt. Gen. Nam Il and Lt. Gen. William K. Harrison at 10:00 A.M. at Panmunjom; twelve hours later the fighting ends.

June 13–15,
Officials of South Korea and North Korea meet in Pyongyang, North Korea, to begin discussions on how to normalize relations between their two countries, a breakthrough conference that opened up new possibilities for the eventual reunification of the two Koreas.

The War Without a Winner

W. Averell Harriman once labeled it "A sour little war."[1] Early in the conflict, Dean Acheson slapped his desk and grumbled, "If the best minds in the world had set out to find us the worst possible location in the world to fight this damnable war, politically and militarily, the unanimous choice would have been Korea."[2] Despite their misgivings about the timing, location, and character of the Korean War, both Harriman, a veteran diplomat and longtime U.S. ambassador to the Soviet Union, and Acheson, President Harry Truman's secretary of state, played important roles in shaping U.S. policy in the conflict.

Many other Americans also thought Korea was an unlikely and inhospitable place to send their soldiers to fight just five years after the end of World War II. In his book *In Mortal Combat*, however, historian John Toland writes that the eruption of Korean hostilities on June 25, 1950, when Communist North Korea invaded democratic South Korea, was inevitable. It was, he argues, simply the next battleground in a chain of tragic wars that various nations waged during the twentieth century in a never-ending quest for more territory, power, and economic riches. Toland writes:

World War I, with the crushing defeat of Germany and its Allies, left Europe in a state of chaos, leading to the rise of Nazism, fascism and communism. The inequities of the peace and the violent struggle for power in Europe, together with the dramatic emergence of a modern, aggressive nation in Asia [Japan], spawned World War II. [Adolf] Hitler and his evil cohorts were smashed, but no sooner was this danger eliminated than another arose—the Cold War and the constant threat of nuclear disaster. The offspring of these evolutionary events was the Korean War.[3]

THE FORGOTTEN WAR?

The Korean War is sometimes called "The Forgotten War" because it is overshadowed in historical terms by the conflicts that occurred before and after it, World War II and the Vietnam War. But another reason for the negative nickname is that most Americans *wanted* to forget this war as soon as it was over because it became the first military struggle America failed to win.

When the two sides signed a truce on July 27, 1953, there were no wild outpourings of joy, no parades for returning military heroes who had conquered yet another enemy threatening America. There was simply a weary sense of relief that American troops were no longer dying in the bitter fighting of an unpopular war. Even Toland, whose *In Mortal Combat* is one of the finest books written about the Korean War, admits that he had a similar reaction:

After two cataclysmic world conflicts [World War I and World War II], it [the

A wounded U.S. Marine awaits help during the Korean War, a conflict Americans wanted to forget because it was the first military struggle the United States failed to win.

Korean War] appeared to be lackluster in global importance and dramatic interest. At the time I shared the popular dislike of this war. Drained by World War II, I, like so many Americans, blocked out the three tedious years of this struggle. Our interests were in our own recovery and that of Europe, not dangerous involvement in the Orient.[4]

Despite the fact that the significance of Harriman's "sour little war" has often been overlooked, the conflict marked a watershed moment in world history; democratic nations, led by the United States, were finally willing to take up arms to stop a Communist military takeover. In *Korea: The Unknown War*, military historians Jon Halliday and Bruce Cumings write:

> The Korean War was the most important war ever fought between the West and Communism. It saw sixteen armies from all five continents deployed under U.S. command. It brought the people of Korea appalling destruction, devastation and tragedy; there were millions of deaths and more millions of divided families; yet it is still an unknown war, with unraveled mysteries and continuing evasions by the major belligerents. Both sides claim to have won, yet both actually seem to feel they lost.[5]

A PRESIDENTIAL HISTORIAN

While the Korean War was raging, it carried another nickname, "Truman's War," be-cause it was President Truman who almost single-handedly decided that America had to help South Korea when it was invaded. When Truman learned of the invasion, his mind flashed back to similar incidents of aggression leading up to World War II, when Germany and Japan, unchecked by the rest of the world, brazenly invaded and conquered their neighboring nations. Truman wrote years later that:

> I had remembered how each time that the democracies failed to act, it encouraged the aggressors to keep going ahead. If the Communists were permitted to force their way into the Republic of Korea without opposition from the free world, no small nation would have the courage to resist threats and aggression by their Communist neighbors. If this was allowed to go unchallenged, it would mean a Third World War, just as similar incidents had brought on the Second World War.[6]

When World War II finally ended, Truman, like people the world over, had hoped it would be the last they would ever experience. But even before the fighting stopped, the Union of Soviet Socialist Republics (U.S.S.R.) and its Communist philosophy emerged as a new American foe. Although the Cold War between the world's reigning superpowers over the next four decades was primarily a diplomatic and ideological conflict, it would erupt several times into full-scale war. The first military engagement was June 25, 1950. "The attack upon Korea," Truman

Nazi Germany's unchecked aggression before World War II was a main factor in President Truman's decision to send U.S. troops to Korea.

declared, "makes it plain beyond all doubt that Communism has passed beyond the use of subversion [unfair tactics] to conquer independent nations and will now use armed invasion and war."[7]

Truman believed that the bitter lessons learned in World War II dictated only one response—to fight back. And he was ready to commit American military might to that battle.

Chapter 1

The Cold War Begins

On March 5, 1946, former British prime minister Winston Churchill uttered a phrase at Westminster College in Fulton, Missouri, that would resonate grimly through the remainder of the twentieth century. "From Stettin in the Baltic to Trieste in the Adriatic," Churchill told an audience that included President Harry S. Truman, "an Iron Curtain has descended across the [European] Continent."[8] In another speech the following year in Columbia, South Carolina, Bernard Baruch, a U.S. diplomat, coined another term to describe the deteriorating relations between the United States and the Union of Soviet Socialist Republics (U.S.S.R.). "Let us not be deceived," Baruch said, "today we are in the midst of a Cold War."[9]

For nearly a half century those two short, simple phrases—Iron Curtain and Cold War—would sum up the battle of ideas the two enemies were waging around the world. The *Iron Curtain* symbolized the loss of freedom that people living in Eastern Europe experienced when the Soviet Union forced them to accept Communist rule after World War II. The *Cold War* was the battle for supremacy between the Soviet Union's and America's radically different political and economic beliefs. This conflict was usually waged through propaganda and donations of economic and military aid to other countries, but it sometimes flared into a shooting, or "hot," war, as in Korea and, a decade later, in Vietnam, another Asian nation split in half by the ongoing conflict between Communism and democracy.

THE POSTWAR WORLD

The seeds that bore the bitter fruit of the Cold War and the Korean War were sown in World War II. They were the dramatic destruction and devastation that accompanied the twentieth century's most horrific global conflict. With the exception of the United States, which was almost untouched by World War II's devastation, the Allied victors paid a terrible price to defeat Germany and Japan. Although the economic and social structures of those two nations were destroyed by ground warfare and devastating bombing, including two nuclear bombs dropped on Japan, a disaster of similar proportions befell Great Britain, France, and other European countries as well as Pacific and Asian nations such as the Philippines, Korea, and China.

In *The Shaping of the American Past*, historian Robert Kelley explains some of the dire postwar conditions:

> Europe was in a state of collapse. Its railroads, factories, electrical systems, banking houses, supplies of capital, farms, markets—all had been utterly devastated by the war. The governments of each European country staggered from crisis to crisis, overwhelmed by millions of refugees, desperately trying to feed starving populations and unable to find capital anywhere.[10]

When Germany surrendered on May 7, 1945, Soviet troops were left in physical control of half of defeated Germany as well as nine previously independent Eastern European countries including Poland, Czechoslovakia, and Hungary. In a series of wartime conferences, the major Allied leaders—President Franklin D. Roosevelt, Churchill, and Soviet premier Joseph Stalin—had promised that when the fighting ended, people living in occupied territories could freely choose new governments for their shattered countries.

But when Stalin refused to honor his commitment and, instead, forcibly installed Communist regimes in occupied Soviet areas, American officials, fearing that Europe's future was at stake, decided they must meet the Communist challenge. Thus was born the struggle that would dominate

London after a bombing during World War II. With the exception of the United States, the Allied victors paid a terrible price to defeat Germany and Japan.

world affairs in the second half of the twentieth century. In *The Wars of America*, Robert Leckie writes that when World War II ended, there was no real peace:

> Because the purpose of war is not merely to defeat the enemy but to ensure a better and more lasting peace, the war ended in tragic failure. [The Soviet Union] and America, which had emerged from the war as [the world's only] superpowers, could not [resolve] their differences and make common cause for world peace; for the wreckage of the German and Japanese empires had left a power vacuum into which [the Soviet Union] rushed and where she was finally confronted by the United States. Thus was begun the Cold War.[11]

FROM ENEMIES TO ALLIES

An old saying states that "The enemy of my enemy is my friend." It was this convoluted diplomatic logic that united the Soviet Union and United States against Adolf Hitler's Nazi Germany. But it was an uneasy alliance from the start because their contrasting political and economic systems had previously divided the two nations for three decades.

When the Communists overthrew Russian czar Nicholas II in 1917 and their political preaching contributed to violent disorder in other European nations following World War I, Americans began to fear that this strange new ideology could endanger their own country. Communism is a totalitarian form of government in which the state owns and controls all segments of the economy. As such, it is directly opposed to America's system of democracy and capitalism, a financial model based on private ownership of property and a free economy.

Heightened by postwar labor strife and a backlash against the millions of immigrants who had journeyed to America in the early 1900s seeking a better way of life, a fear of Communism dubbed the "Red Scare" swept the United States. In 1919, U.S. attorney general A. Mitchell Palmer had thousands of people arrested who belonged to the fledgling Communist Party as well as other radical political and labor groups, because the government believed their new social ideas could harm America. Even though most were never found guilty of any crimes, hundreds of innocent people, including many children, were deported (sent back) to their former countries.

This adversarial relationship changed dramatically during World War II. America's onetime enemy became an admired ally by valiantly resisting a massive Nazi invasion, tying up millions of German soldiers who had invaded the Soviet Union and making it easier for the United States, Great Britain, and other Allied nations to attack Germany in Europe. The United States sent the Soviet Union hundreds of millions of dollars in food, medical supplies, and weapons, and Americans were awed by the bravery and fierce fighting ability of Soviet soldiers. During the war, President Franklin D. Roosevelt once commented playfully that the Soviets might not be "housebroken" but "were a very good breed of dog."[12]

SOVIETS BECOME HEROES IN AMERICA

One of the most amazing developments of World War II was the speed with which the Soviet Union was transformed from an enemy into a trusted, respected American ally. In his book The Cold War: A History, *Martin Walker comments on the depth of the American acceptance of its former rival:*

"There are few things harder to comprehend than the extraordinary popularity in the West by 1945 of 'Uncle Joe' Stalin and the heroic Red Army. For the American public, immune behind the Atlantic barrier, and for the British behind the Channel, there was something epic about the way the Red Army had borne the brunt of the fighting against [Adolf] Hitler's [army] . . . until the U.S. and British troops invaded Italy in 1943, [the other Allied nations] were facing only four divisions of German troops, while the Red Army grappled with more than two hundred. Even for many conservatives, the pre-war memories of the evils of Communism had been redeemed by the blood the Red Army had shed in four years of war. As wartime allies, the Russians were hailed as 'one hell of a people, who look like Americans, dress like Americans and think like Americans,' by the later passionately anti-Soviet *Life* magazine. *Fortune* [magazine] ran an opinion poll in 1943 which found 81 percent of the respondents agreeing that the U.S. should work with Russia as equal partners in the coming peace."

American and Soviet troops exchange handshakes and smiles in Germany.

THE COLD WAR BEGINS

This unlikely friendship forged through war, however, began to break down before the fighting ended. Most historians date the start of the Cold War to the Yalta Conference, a meeting of Roosevelt, Churchill, and Stalin from February 4–12, 1945, in the Crimea, the ancient Black Sea resort of Russian czars. With Germany on the brink of defeat, the

Big Three, as they were known to the world, met to plan how to reorganize the postwar world.

At Yalta all three leaders agreed to honor the Declaration on Liberated Europe, which ensured "the right of all peoples to choose the form of government under which they will live [and] the restoration of sovereign rights and self-government to those peoples who have been forcibly deprived of them by the aggressor nations."[13] But Stalin never intended to honor the agreement and instead decided to keep the land his troops had conquered in battle. Explaining why he acted as he did, Stalin once said, "This war is not as in the past. Whoever occupies a ter-

ritory also imposes on it his own social system. Everybody imposes his own system as far as his army can reach. It cannot be otherwise."[14]

At Yalta, Roosevelt was sick and weary, still weakened by a stroke suffered the previous summer and only a few weeks away from the final, fatal seizure that would take his life. The president's illness is one reason he may have failed to realize Stalin's true motives, but in *A History of the American People*, Paul Johnson offers a second explanation for Roosevelt's failure to understand Stalin:

> While often subtle and sometimes shrewd about American domestic poli-

Pictured (left to right) at the Yalta Conference are the Big Three: Winston Churchill, Franklin D. Roosevelt, and Joseph Stalin.

Joseph Stalin: "A Moral Cripple"

George F. Kennan was one of the most influential U.S. officials in shaping America's response to the Soviet challenge following World War II, including the decision to defend South Korea when it was attacked in 1950. An expert on the Soviet Union who met Premier Joseph Stalin many times over several decades, Kennan understood the leaders as well as any American of his time. In his 1996 book At a Century's Ending: Reflections, 1982–1995, *Kennan discusses Stalin's strengths and weaknesses:*

"Stalin did have certain exceptional and highly remarkable talents. Outstanding among these were: (1) an almost diabolic ability to sense, and to see into, the innermost thoughts and motivations of persons near to him; (2) a truly impressive tactical skill in the manipulation of others, both as individuals and in groups; and (3) a capacity for dissimulation for which even the greatest of performing actors might have envied him. His inadequacies in other respects were no less remarkable than his talents. To be born, as he was, without the capacity for either shame or pity (and we might add to that list: loyalty) was a very real deprivation (like his withered arm). It was a species of birth defect. He was in that sense born a moral cripple. And the effect of this, superimposed on the exceptional talents that he did have, was appalling. This combination of the negative capacities he had and the positive ones he lacked was plainly a devil's brew, out of which arose some of the greatest disasters of the century now passing."

tics, he [Roosevelt] was extremely naive, and sometimes woefully ignorant about [international] political strategy. In particular, he tended, like many intellectuals and pseudo-intellectuals of his time, to take the Soviet Union at its face value—a peace-loving "People's Democracy," with an earnest desire to better the conditions of the working people of the world.[15]

At Yalta the Big Three made many important decisions. They agreed to form an international peacekeeping organization, a body that would eventually become the United Nations; to partition Germany into four occupation zones, make it pay war reparations, and render it incapable of ever making war again; to try Nazi war criminals; and to hold free elections in occupied countries. They also entered into a secret pact in which Churchill and Roosevelt promised Stalin the return of territory his country had lost during its 1904 war with Japan—the Kurile Islands and land in Manchuria—if the Soviet Union would help defeat Japan.

Although Roosevelt has been harshly criticized for making agreements favorable to the Soviet Union, he was not the only American who believed that the Soviets would remain an ally when the fighting stopped. A June 1945 Gallup Poll showed that more than half of U.S. citizens thought the Soviet Union would honor commitments it made at Yalta and other wartime conferences.

Historians also believe Roosevelt was overly generous because he naively believed that if he were nice to Stalin, the U.S.S.R would help in the postwar task of rebuilding a free world, would help to defeat Japan, which Roosevelt's military advisers believed was important to limit U.S. deaths, and would join the planned new United Nations, which Roosevelt believed could ensure future world peace. "I think that if I give him [Stalin] everything I possibly can and ask nothing from him in return," Roosevelt once said, "he won't try to annex anything and will work with me for a world of democracy and peace."[16]

Roosevelt's faith in Stalin would prove to be unwarranted. And Robert Leckie as well as many other historians claim that the agreements Roosevelt made at Yalta had disastrous future consequences for the entire world:

> At Yalta were made the concessions and agreements which enabled Stalin to place Communist puppets in Poland and to undermine opposition to the Red takeovers planned for central Europe and the Balkans. Yalta also made the Soviet Union an Asiatic power at the expense of [Chinese Nationalist leader] Chiang Kai-shek and paved the way for the rise of Chinese Communist leader Mao Tse-tung.[17]

While Stalin was making meaningless promises at Yalta, Soviet troops in Poland and other Soviet-occupied countries were suppressing non-Communist political groups and establishing Soviet-controlled Communist governments. Within a few weeks after Yalta ended, however, U.S. officials began to realize what Stalin was doing. On April 6, just six days before Roosevelt died, W. Averell Harriman, the U.S. ambassador to the Soviet Union, sent a lengthy cablegram to the State Department in which he exposed Stalin's true postwar intentions:

> We now have ample proof that the Soviet government views all matters from the standpoint of their own selfish interest. We must clearly recognize that the Soviet program is the establishment of totalitarianism, ending personal liberty and democracy as we know it and respect it.[18]

There is evidence that if Roosevelt had lived, he would have been more wary in his dealings with the Soviet premier. "Averell is right," Roosevelt said at Warm Springs, Georgia, the health spa where he was trying to regain his strength. "We can't do business with Stalin."[19] Tragically, Roosevelt's awareness of Soviet treachery came too late. A few days later, he died.

A NEW PRESIDENT

On April 12, 1945, Harry S. Truman was summoned to the White House and told by Eleanor Roosevelt that her husband had died. Truman became president under tragic circumstances at a pivotal and dangerous point in U.S. history. In his first meet-

PRESIDENT HARRY S. TRUMAN

Harry S. Truman, the thirty-third president of the United States, faced a difficult situation when Franklin D. Roosevelt died. America had still not defeated Germany or Japan and was facing growing problems in its relations with the Soviet Union. But in A History of the American People, *Paul Johnson claims that Truman, who when he became president was not well-known or highly regarded by many Americans, was exactly the leader the nation needed in such perilous times:*

"Harry S. Truman proved to be one of the great American presidents, and in some respects the most typical. He was seen at the time of his sudden precipitation into the White House as a nonentity, a machine-man, a wholly parochial and selfish politician from a backward border state who would be lost in the world of international statesmanship in which he now became the leading player. In fact Truman acquitted himself well, almost from the start, and not only the United States but the whole world had reason to be grateful for his simple, old-fashioned sense of justice, the clear distinctions he drew between right and wrong, and the decisiveness with which he applied them to the immense global problems which confronted him from the very first moments of his presidency."

ing with reporters after Roosevelt's death, Truman admitted how crushing his new responsibilities were: "Boys, if you ever pray for me, pray for me now. When they told me yesterday what had happened, I felt as though the moon, stars, and all the planets had fallen upon me."[20]

At first many Americans wondered if Truman would be capable of handling the huge tasks facing him: leading the nation to final victory over Japan, dealing with the growing Soviet menace to freedom in the rest of the world, and guiding America successfully into the postwar era. The reason for this doubt was his humble background. The son of a mule trader and farmer, Truman's formal education in his hometown of Independence, Missouri, had ended with high

school. Although he was the last American president who did not attend college, he kept learning by reading widely, especially history. Truman fought in World War I, became a partner in a men's clothing store in Kansas City, and when his business failed during the Great Depression he turned to politics. Serving first as a county judge, Truman in 1935 won a U.S. Senate seat and in 1944 was elected vice president.

But this unassuming Midwesterner would prove that he was worthy to be president and would impress many people with his willingness to take responsibility for all of his actions, a characteristic he defined with the homespun phrase, "The buck stops here."[21] Noted historians Allan Nevins and Henry Steele Commager write that Truman quickly showed he was capable of dealing with the many difficult tasks he confronted:

> Events soon proved that Truman had remarkable qualifications for not only national but international leadership. . . . He believed fervently in action and leadership. And when crises came, this peaceable-looking man rose with instant decision and fierce fighting power to meet them.[22]

Truman's ability to make tough decisions was put to the test only months after he took office. He had to decide whether or not to use a terrible new weapon the United States had developed—the atomic bomb.

The city of Nagasaki as it appeared after the dropping of the atomic bomb.

THE ATOMIC BOMB

In April 1945, Hitler's armies were collapsing and it was only a matter of weeks before Germany would surrender. But even though it was apparent that Germany's ally, Japan, had also lost the war, its soldiers continued to wage a bloody defensive battle and its government created "Operation Decision," an all-encompassing plan to have soldiers and civilians fight to the death when the Allies invaded their homeland.

Truman and other American leaders were worried that hundreds of thousands of U.S. soldiers would die or be wounded in such an invasion, but there would be no need for this final, bloody battle. When Truman became the nation's leader, he was informed of the atomic bomb, a weapon developed in such secrecy that even as vice president he had not been told of it. After the the United States successfully exploded the first atomic bomb on July 12 in New Mexico, govern-

ment officials moved swiftly to warn the Japanese that they faced an immensely powerful new weapon and demanded the nation's unconditional surrender. When the Japanese refused, Truman ordered that an atomic bomb be dropped on Japan. The city of Hiroshima was the target.

Although the devastating blast on August 6 killed eighty thousand people and destroyed Hiroshima, the Japanese still refused to give up. In response, Truman ordered a second nuclear attack three days later on another Japanese city, Nagasaki. The destructive force of this second atomic bomb killed more than forty thousand people and forced Japan to surrender. A cease-fire went into effect on August 15 and two weeks later the Japanese signed documents ending the war.

The decision to use the most deadly weapon ever created was difficult. But the feisty new president believed he had no choice; the bomb would end the war a year early and spare the lives of tens of thousands of American soldiers who would die during an invasion of Japan. Truman said,

> As president of the United States, I had the fateful responsibility of deciding whether or not to use the atom bomb for the first time. It was the hardest decision I ever had to make. But the president cannot duck hard problems—he cannot pass the buck. . . . We have used it [the atom bomb] in order to shorten the agony of war, in order to save the lives of thousands and thousands of young Americans.[23]

TRUMAN GETS TOUGH

From July 17 to August 2, only a few weeks before the war in the Pacific ended, Truman, Stalin, and Churchill met in the German city of Potsdam, a suburb of Berlin, to make more decisions about postwar life in Europe. But unlike Roosevelt, Truman was suspicious of Stalin's true intentions from the start; the new president had always believed that the Soviet Union was "essentially a gangster state" and that Stalin was "as untrustworthy as Hitler or [U.S. gangster] Al Capone."[24]

Truman had first displayed this new U.S. attitude toward the Soviets several months earlier in an April 30 White House meeting with Vyacheslav Molotov, the Soviet Union's foreign minister. The blunt-spoken Truman told Molotov he was angry that the Soviets had not kept their agreement to allow Poland and other occupied nations to freely choose new governments. "I gave it to him straight," Truman recalled years later. "I let him have it. It was the straight one-two to the jaw."[25] Molotov was shocked at the direct, an-

gry message, saying, "I have never been talked to like that in my life," to which Truman snapped, "Carry out your agreements and you won't get talked to like that!"[26]

When Truman arrived in Potsdam he knew Stalin was continuing to ignore his Yalta promises; that Romania, Hungary, and Bulgaria were already controlled by Communists; and that the Soviets were stripping those occupied areas of raw materials. They dismantled industries and even ripped out toilets and other plumbing fixtures, shipping them back to the Soviet Union to rebuild their own shattered homeland.

At Potsdam, Stalin was adamant in his refusal to let the Allies interfere in Eastern Europe, a belligerent attitude that destroyed the goodwill that had prevailed at previous conferences. "We are asking for the reorganization of the satellite governments [the Eastern European nations the Communists had taken over] along democratic lines as agreed upon at Yalta," Truman bluntly told Stalin, to which the Soviet premier blandly replied, "If a government is not fascist, a government is democratic."[27]

Truman knew that Communism, a form of government that drastically limits its citizens' freedom, was not democratic. Yet Stalin could blithely insist that it *was* democratic simply because it was not fascist.

THE COLD WAR BEGINS

And so, before the grim echoes of World War II had faded away, the United States and the Soviet Union drifted into another conflict. Historian Robert Kelley writes that Americans were angry at the Soviets for denying them, as well as people in the rest

Their Pasts Shaped America and Russia

Many people wonder why the United States and the Union of Soviet Socialist Republics became such bitter enemies after being allies in World War II. In The Shaping of the American Past, *Robert Kelley explains that the radically different pasts of the two nations, and how those events shaped their perspectives, is what divided them:*

"Russia and America were profoundly different in their national experiences, and in their basic values and ideas. Out of these differences sprang inevitable disagreement. By 1945, the American people had had many generations of internal stability.... [America] was a successful country, affluent, and relatively untouched by World War II. . . . As the first democratic nation, the United States of America was inspired by a dream of carrying its national ideology, democracy, to the world at large. Its citizens assumed that the wave of the future was with them and with their way of living. What could be more natural, Americans felt, than that all peoples should be allowed the right democratically to choose and run their own governments, with guarantees (as in the United States) of basic human rights?

Russia is an ancient country [that] has been invaded again and again in its long history.... Consequently, the Russians were not in 1945 a trusting people.... The Russians have felt surrounded by enemies since long before the Communist revolution took place under V. I. Lenin in 1917. In 1945, much of the USSR lay in shattered, smoking ruins, and the Soviets were determined to guarantee their future military security by their own efforts, not by trusting others. It would be inconceivable, in their minds, to stand back in the countries their armies now occupied in Eastern and Central Europe and allow Western-style democratic regimes—capitalist and middle- and upper-class dominated—to take over. The memory of two massive German invasions since 1914 also made [them] believe that . . . the countries in Slavic Europe through which the German armies had come (Poland, Czechoslovakia, Hungary, Rumania, and the Balkans), must be directly under their control so that such invasions could never occur again."

of the world, the peace that everyone desired following a long, bloody war, and that this powerful emotion helped push the United States into a new worldwide battle:

They were bitter, therefore, toward the Soviets. Americans took up the Cold War with a grim obsessiveness and self-righteousness that produced a near wartime national atmosphere. Used to thinking of great crusades, they hated this new enemy and thirsted for its complete destruction.[28]

2 The Cold War Turns Hot in Korea

An ancient Korean proverb claims, "A shrimp is crushed in the battle of the whales."[29] And so it was throughout the long history of Korea, which had the misfortune to lie at a geographical and political crossroads in Asia that saw the nation repeatedly invaded by stronger neighbors. In 1592 the Japanese leader Toyotomi Hideyoshi used Korea as a route to attack China, only to be defeated in a six-year war. China later invaded Korea in 1632, forcing that country to acknowledge its supremacy and heavily influencing its affairs for several centuries.

During the nineteenth century, Russia, which became the Soviet Union after the 1917 Communist revolution, also became a power in Asia. When that occurred, Russia and later the Soviet Union began a historic triangular conflict with China and Japan for control of Korea. During its 1904 war with Russia, Japan forcibly took control of Korea and ruled it for the next four decades.

When Japan was defeated in World War II, it appeared that Korea would finally have a chance to govern itself again. But the growing Cold War rivalry between the United States and the Soviet Union would doom Korean hopes for freedom and lead to the division of this ancient land.

KOREA IS DIVIDED

It was not until the war in the Pacific was almost over that Premier Joseph Stalin honored his Yalta commitment to battle Japan, and then, in the view of most historians, he did so only to make sure that the U.S.S.R. could grab its share of the former Japanese empire. "Aware that they faced a race against time if any of the spoils of war were to be won," Martin Walker explains in *The Cold War: A History*, "the Soviet Union declared war [against Japan] on August 9, the day the second atom bomb fell on Nagasaki."[30] It was a decision that would prove disastrous for Korea.

Soviet troops immediately advanced into Chinese Manchuria and the northern tip of Korea, a Japanese possession since 1910. Meeting only minor resistance, Stalin ordered his army to seize as much territory as it could in Korea as quickly as possible in order to establish a Communist presence, the same tactic he had used to take control of Eastern European nations. Aware that the onrushing Soviets were trying to secure territory they might never relinquish, U.S. officials realized that they, too, had to stake a claim to part of Korea and decided to establish a line in the country where the two armies would meet to accept the surrender of the Japanese.

Shortly after midnight on August 11, two young army colonels, Dean Rusk and Charles H. Bonesteel, began deciding how to divide Korea. Working with a sketchy map that gave them only the barest outlines of a land they had never seen, their superior, John J. McCloy of the State-War-Navy Coordinating Committee, gave them only thirty minutes to make a decision that would dramatically alter Korea's future and influence events in Asia for the rest of the century. Speed was a necessity because the U.S. military was rushing to complete its plans for Japan's surrender, an event officials expected to occur at any time.

Rusk and Bonesteel soon noted that the 38th parallel effectively divided Korea in half and could become a sensible border between the two territories. Rusk, who as secretary of defense during the 1960s would help guide U.S. policy in the Vietnam War, commented years later on why he and Bonesteel chose the 38th parallel:

> The military view was that if our proposals for receiving the surrender greatly over-reached our probable military capabilities [of securing that area], there would be little likelihood of Soviet acceptance—and speed was the essence of the problem. Even though [the line] was further north than could be realistically reached by U.S. forces in the event of Soviet disagreement . . . we felt it important to include the capital of Korea [Seoul] in the area of responsibility of American troops.[31]

NORTH AND SOUTH KOREA

When U.S. officials proposed this division to the Soviets, they at first feared they might have tried to claim too much territory—the United States, after all, did not have any troops in Korea and the first Americans would not land there until September 9—but the Soviets accepted the demarcation without hesitation. The two halves of Korea now divided by the 38th parallel became known as North and South Korea.

The division left the south with 37,000 square miles and about 21 million people, two-thirds of them farm families in a bountiful agricultural area that grew enough rice to feed the entire nation. The north had only about 9 million residents but at 48,000 square miles was larger and much more industrialized, home to most of Korea's hydroelectric plants and its chemical, steel, cement, and fertilizer industries.

Although the demarcation decision was made easily, almost casually, historian Doug Dowd writes that, "From the moment of its establishment as a dividing line, the 38th parallel took on a life of its own, and became a looming Frankenstein monster."[32] Ultimately, it was a decision that would lead directly to the Korean War.

THE TRUMAN DOCTRINE

Although U.S. troops occupied half of divided Korea following World War II, America's main Cold War focus was on Europe, the area of the world where U.S. officials most feared that Communist takeovers would occur. It was during this period that President Harry S. Truman began taking an increasingly hard stance against Communism. On January 5, 1946, he wrote in his diary, "I do not think we should play compromise any longer. . . . I am tired of babying the Soviets."[33] The United States, however, would have to confront the Soviet Union almost single-handedly, because Great Britain and its other European allies were so devastated by war that they could not contribute many resources to the battle.

Before World War II, Great Britain had controlled a colonial empire that stretched around the globe and been the primary peacekeeper when trouble arose in various areas of the world. But in early 1947 the British told U.S. officials their country no longer had enough money to support forces in Greece and Turkey that were battling Communist-led groups seeking control of those nations. Faced with the prospect of losing the two countries to Communism, Truman decided the United States had to back them. In a speech to Congress on March 12, 1947, Truman asked for $400 million to help Greece and Turkey rebuild their nations and strengthen their armies to resist Communist aggression. Said Truman:

> The seeds of totalitarian regimes are nurtured by misery and want. They spread and grow in the evil soil of poverty and strife. They reach their full growth when the hope of a people for a better life has died. We must keep that hope alive. I believe that it must be the policy of the United States to support free peoples who are resisting attempted subjugation by armed minorities or by outside pressures.[34]

Truman's decision to provide economic and military aid to foreign nations so they could remain free became known as the *Truman Doctrine*, a policy that formally committed the United States to fighting Communism around the world and signaled a key shift in global power, with the United States replacing Great Britain as the world's protector. America, which for most of its existence had remained isolated from other countries, would now extend a helping hand wherever it was needed to fight Communism or enable weaker nations to become stronger.

THE MARSHALL PLAN

The assistance helped democratic governments in Greece and Turkey survive. But Truman and his newly-named secretary of state, former army general George Marshall, soon realized that even countries with long histories of freedom could fall to Communism due to enormous postwar economic problems. In a speech on June 5, 1947, at the Harvard University commencement, Marshall unveiled a new strategy that became known as the *Marshall Plan*, a wide-ranging program that would channel $12 billion in U.S. aid to Europe. Said Marshall:

> Our policy is not directed against any country or doctrine, but is directed against hunger, poverty, desperation, and chaos. Its purpose should be the revival of a working economy in the world so as to permit the emergence of political and economic conditions in which free institutions can exist.[35]

In late 1947, when Truman asked Congress to fund the Marshall Plan (which was officially called the Eastern Europe Economic Recovery Program), some congressmen ridiculed it as the "great giveaway" because they did not think the aid was necessary to fight Communism. But when the Soviet Union staged a brutal coup d'état in Czechoslovakia in February 1948, forcing the once-free nation to turn Communist, Congress was jolted into action.

It approved the Marshall Plan on April 3 and for the next four years financial aid flowed to sixteen European nations, allowing war-ravaged countries such as France and Italy to recover economically and remain democratic. The only Communist nation the United States helped was Yugoslavia, which was ruled by Marshal Tito, a Communist leader who refused to take orders from the Soviet Union. U.S. officials helped Yugoslavia because they wanted to remain on friendly terms with Tito.

The Marshall Plan was the practical extension of the Containment Policy, an anti-Communist strategy first outlined in a July 1947 article in *Foreign Affairs* magazine by an author identified only as "X." The author was actually George F. Kennan, a veteran State Department official stationed in the Soviet Union, who argued that America had to stop Communism from spreading.

The article was a public statement of views that Kennan had first articulated to U.S. officials a year earlier in what was called the "long telegram," which he had sent from Moscow. In the magazine article, Kennan argued that, "It is clear the main element of any United States policy toward the Soviet Union must be that of a long-term, patient but firm and vigilant containment of Russian expansive tendencies."[36]

THE MARSHALL PLAN

One of the key weapons the United States and Soviet Union employed in the Cold War was economic aid to other countries, either to sway them to their side or to strengthen governments already favorable to them. The early centerpiece of this U.S. tactic was the Marshall Plan. In The Shaping of the American Past, *Robert Kelley explains how it helped Europe recover from World War II:*

"The Marshall Plan aimed essentially at creating a prosperous and therefore contented Europe. How? By giving large redevelopment funds outright to the European nations; reducing and eventually breaking down all barriers to trade, nation to nation; reforming Europe's currencies so that they were freely convertible, one to another; and building a structure of Europe-wide political institutions that would link together and coordinate its economic life. These steps, as historian Michael J. Hogan has written, were to 'set the stage for security and recovery [in Europe] and for a [new] system of world trade.' The Marshall Plan turned out to be one of those historic rarities; a strikingly innovative public policy that was astonishingly successful."

Secretary of State George Marshall, author of the Marshall Plan, which helped European countries' recovery after World War II.

THE COLD WAR HEATS UP

Although by 1948 the Cold War was already several years old, the two opponents had never directly confronted each other. That changed on June 24, 1948, when the Soviets began an armed blockade to keep western forces out of Berlin, Germany's former capital. When World War II ended, the Allies had divided Germany into four zones of occupation that were governed individually by America, Great Britain, France, and the Soviet Union. Berlin was entirely within the Soviet-occupied eastern part of Germany, but the capital city itself had also been divided into four similar occupation zones.

Angry that a bastion of democracy survived in the midst of the Communist nation it was building, the Soviets shut down access to Berlin via train or automobile, turning back western shipments of food,

A U.S. plane brings in supplies to West Berlin during the Berlin Airlift.

medicine, fuel, coal, and other necessities people in the non-Soviet sectors needed to survive. The Soviets hoped this tactic would allow them to control Berlin completely, but the United States and Great Britain answered with a massive airlift, one that over eleven months flew in 1.5 million tons of supplies to keep West Berlin's two million people fed, warm, and healthy through a bitter winter. The blockade ended on May 12, 1949, after the Soviets finally realized their plan had failed.

U.S. elation over beating the Berlin blockade, however, was counterbalanced by two Communist triumphs that fall which shocked and depressed Americans. In a September 29 news conference, Truman admitted the United States no longer had a monopoly on atomic weapons: "We have evidence that . . . an atomic explosion has occurred in the U.S.S.R."[37] And on October 1, Chairman Mao Tse-tung proclaimed the formation of the People's Republic of China after his army defeated Nationalist forces led by Chiang Kai-shek. The two sides had waged a civil war since the 1920s, battling each other even after the Japanese invaded China in 1937. U.S. officials had backed the Nationalists because Chiang's government was anti-Communist.

The fact that China had turned Communist was a severe blow to the United States, which had given the Nationalists $2 billion in economic and military aid. President Truman was bitterly attacked by Republicans and others for having "lost China," but in *A History of the American People*, author Paul Johnson writes, "The truth is China lost itself."[38] Johnson and other historians note that Chiang's government was corrupt, its officials stealing hundreds of millions of dollars in U.S. aid for private purposes, and that the Communists triumphed because they were able to win the support of more Chinese citizens. After their defeat the Nationalists moved to an island off the coast of mainland China called Formosa (now Taiwan) and established their own government, which they called the Republic of China.

KOREA: AN ANCIENT NATION

The fall of China meant that Korea had a Communist neighbor, one big enough and powerful enough to gobble it up at will. But Korea had faced the threat of invasion and subjugation throughout recorded history, extending back to its emergence as the Kingdom of Silla during the seventh century A.D. In *Korea: The Unknown War*, authors Jon Halliday and Bruce Cumings explain:

Korea is one of the oldest nations on earth, with a rich culture, more than a millennium of unity, and an indisputable national identity. . . . Deeply influenced by neighboring China [from which it absorbed its writing system, laws, and fine arts], its foreign policy [for many centuries] was one of strict seclusion, which led to the country being known as the "Hermit Kingdom." For a quarter century after 1876, the peninsula was the object of rivalry among Russia, Japan, the United States and Britain. Japan ended this rivalry by defeating Russia in their 1905 war and made Korea a colony in 1910.[39]

The Korean peninsula extends southward from what used to be called Manchuria (now the Chinese provinces of Liaoning, Kirin, and Heilungkiang) and Siberia, Russia's ancient Asian colony. Some 600 miles long and ranging from 125 to 200 miles wide, Korea is a rugged, mountainous nation, approximately the size of New York State, that is bordered on the west by the Yellow Sea and on the east by the Sea of Japan. The name by which Korea is best known to its own people is Choson, which is translated as "Land of the Morning Freshness." The western name of "Korea" was derived from its Koryo dynasty, which ruled from A.D. 935 to 1392.

Korea was a dependent state of China from 1632 until 1895, when Japanese troops defeated Chinese soldiers in yet another of their many military clashes, giving Japan an important new role in Korea's affairs. In 1904, Japan and Russia went to war for control of Korea and Manchuria, with Japan launching a surprise attack on the Russian fleet at Port Arthur. The 1905 peace treaty, which was negotiated in the United States with the help of President Theodore Roosevelt, left Japan in charge of Korea, and five years later it formally annexed that country.

A JAPANESE COLONY

From 1910 until the end of World War II, Japan ruled Korea brutally. Although Japan helped modernize the once-backward nation, it also tried to wipe out Korean culture, history, and language to make its people more dependent on Japan. One of Japan's first acts was to force King Kojong to abdicate, ending the Choson dynasty which had ruled since 1392 and eliminating a possible future threat to its rule. In *Korea: The Unknown War*, Halliday and Cumings describe this period:

Japan held Korea for nearly half a century, pursuing a colonialism that both destroyed and created: obliterating Korea's national independence and its self-governing state while building a modern bureaucracy, discriminating against Ko-

---

KOREA

North and South Korea were not created until 1948. But before this ancient nation was artificially divided at the close of World War II, the territory encompassing the two countries had enjoyed a long, rich history. In America in the Korean War, *Edward F. Dolan briefly describes Korea's past:*

"North and South Korea occupy the small Korean peninsula. Bordered by China on the north and Russia on the far northeast, the peninsula stretches southward for 600 miles and measures about 200 miles across at its widest point and some 125 miles at its narrowest. From the farms of each come rice, corn, barley, vegetables, and dairy products. North Korea's principal natural resources are coal, iron, and hydroelectric power. Coal and hydroelectric power are also among South Korea's natural resources, along with lead . . . and graphite. Prior to the division at the 38th parallel, the peninsula was home to the single nation of Korea. . . . The nation's history is thought to date from about 3000 BC. It was ruled by various dynasties until being made a dependent state of China in the seventeenth century. The Chinese reign lasted until the late 1800s, when Japan became the predominant foreign power in Korea. Japan annexed the peninsula in 1910 and then had to give it up after being defeated in World War II."

During the 1937 Japanese invasion of China, hundreds of thousands of Koreans were forced into service to support the Japanese war effort.

reans racially while giving them modern education as good imperial subjects, rewarding collaborators while punishing all but the most moderate forms of resistance, exploiting the economy to Japan's benefit while building an advanced structure of roads, railroads, ports and new industries.[40]

Japan governed Korea's 21 million inhabitants with a large army and a bureaucracy of 246,000 civil servants. A proud people with a long history as a free nation, Korean groups that backed the rights of Koreans to govern their own land rose up several times to resist the Japanese. In March and April of 1919, for example, at least a half-million Koreans took part in more than 600 demonstrations to oppose their colonial bondage. But Japanese authorities brutally repressed the nationalists, arresting at least 12,000 and killing more than 500 to quash the independence movement. In one especially horrible incident, Japanese police locked Korean protesters inside a church and burned it to the ground.

Japan's invasion of China in 1937 marked the start of the harshest period of Japanese rule. To fuel its military machine in Asia before and during World War II, Japan inducted hundreds of thousands of Koreans into its army and forcibly moved almost 2 million citizens to Japan to labor at construction, manufacturing, mining, and agricultural jobs. The greatest horror of this forced labor was a form of sexual slavery in which an estimated 100,000 to 200,000 Korean women had to work as "comfort women," prostitutes in Japanese army brothels.

A convoy of U.S. troops is greeted by joyful students during the liberation of Korea following World War II.

This era is one of the darkest in Korea's long history. In *Korea's Place in the Sun*, Cumings comments on the bitter feelings Koreans still have toward the Japanese:

> Among Koreans today, North and South, the mere mention of the idea that Japan somehow "modernized" Korea calls forth indignant denials. Koreans have always thought that the benefits of [this period] went entirely to Japan and that Korea would have developed rapidly without Japanese help anyway.[41]

KOREA: A DIVIDED LAND

Korea's hope for freedom was raised anew when Allied leaders met in 1943 in Cairo, Egypt. President Franklin D. Roosevelt, Great Britain's Winston Churchill, and Chiang stated in the Cairo Declaration: "Mindful of the enslavement of the Korean people, the aforementioned powers [the United States, Great Britain, and China] are determined Korea shall, in due course, be free and independent."[42]

Allied leaders, however, believed it would take several decades for Korea to learn to govern itself because it had been ruled by Japan for so long. And in August 1945, the United States did not bother to consult any Korean leaders when those two young colonels sliced the country in two along the 38th parallel. Criticized by historians ever since, the decision to partition Korea was not popular in the United States even then. The *New York Herald Tribune* predicted on November 24, 1945, that the artificial line would result in disaster:

SYNGMAN RHEE AND KIM IL SUNG

In Korea: The Untold Story of the War, *Joseph C. Goulden explains that Syngman Rhee and Kim Il Sung were both revolutionaries, although in quite different ways.*

Rhee shed his nation's old-fashioned heritage of academic study and ancestor worship and adopted western ways. He was also so fierce in leading demonstrations demanding an end to Japanese rule that a Seoul newspaper branded him "a radical and a fire-eater," and Japanese officials imprisoned and tortured him. Goulden explains Rhee's transformation:

> "Rhee made what must have been a tremendously difficult decision for a young Asian man. In his late teens he entered a middle school in Seoul run by Methodist missionaries and gradually moved away from the complementary faiths of Buddhism and Confucianism followed by his parents. He cut off the traditional hair topknot worn by Korean males . . . and as he learned about Western democracy, he found the medievalism of Korea's social and political system intolerable. In the space of a few months he made the quantum jump from traditional Orientalism to quasi-Westerner."

Like Rhee, Kim was arrested for working to oust the Japanese. Goulden explains how Kim became a Communist:

> "One guerrilla—the man who was to be the North Korean premier during the Korean War—was born Kim Song-joo . . . in 1912, or so it is stated by modern North Korean propaganda media. No other sources exist. . . . His father, impoverished but bold, taught youngsters [Korean] history and culture by day and trained them to fight the Japanese by night. Arrested and tortured, then driven into exile in Manchuria . . . prison broke his body; he died at thirty-two. Son Kim was said to learn to hate the Japanese early and to have his eyes 'swell with tears' when his mother admonished him to 'grow up fast to avenge your father.'"

Kim became an effective guerrilla fighter and worked all his life for Korean independence. However, Goulden explains that Kim was willing to obey orders from Communist leaders: "Whatever the facts of Kim Il Sung's background, and his wartime career, he clearly was a man the Soviet Union could trust—and control."

There has never been a reasonable excuse for [dividing] a homogenous people. It is creating new political problems. The Koreans are being indoctrinated with Communistic ideas in the north and with theories of Western democracies in the south.[43]

The newspaper editorial's prophecy would come true. The dividing line created two Koreas—one in the south that the United States molded into a democracy, and one in the north that the Communists hammered into yet another Soviet satellite—that would become unalterably opposed to one another.

NORTH AND SOUTH KOREA

A U.S. force of fifty thousand soldiers occupied South Korea from 1945 until 1948, setting up a military government and fostering democracy with $141 million in surplus military matériel and almost $354 million in other economic aid. The Soviets governed the north harshly, eliminating freedom of the press and restricting non-Communist opposition. Although the dual trusteeship was supposed to end with unification, historian Clay Blair claims the way the two occupying nations controlled events destroyed Korea's chance to become whole again: "In sum, the political and economic realities and occupational decisions on the scene in both sectors of Korea were consigning the trusteeship to an early grave."[44]

The United States in September 1947 made one final bid to reunite divided Korea when it asked the United Nations (UN) General Assembly to hold a nationwide election.

The UN agreed to the proposal, which called for withdrawal of all foreign troops after a new national government was chosen.

On May 10, 1948, more than 92 percent of registered voters in the south elected representatives to a new National Assembly, with Syngman Rhee's conservative Korean Democratic Party winning a majority of the legislative seats. On August 15 the seventy-five-year-old Rhee, a respected leader who had worked for Korean independence all his life, was named the first president of the Republic of Korea, which was known in the west as South Korea.

Although the Soviet Union refused to hold elections or allow UN observers to enter the area it controlled, it responded to South Korean elections on September 9 by announcing creation of the Democratic People's Republic of Korea, better known as North Korea, and naming twenty-eight-year-old Kim Il Sung its first premier. Kim was a legendary Communist military leader who had fought the Japanese even before World War II in an effort to win his country's freedom.

The Soviets withdrew their soldiers by the end of 1948, and on the final day of June 1949 the last American troops departed, leaving behind only a group of about five hundred officers and men who would serve as the U.S. Military Advisory Group to the Republic of Korea (KMAG). There were now two Koreas, each guarded by its own army, each dependent upon military help from the two Cold War opponents.

As historian John Toland states, "Korea had become a pawn in the great chess match between the United States and the USSR."[45] War was inevitable.

Chapter

3 North Korea Surprises the World

At a June 1, 1950, news conference, President Harry S. Truman proudly announced that the world was "closer to real peace than at any time in the last five years," and on June 20, Dean Rusk, one of the young colonels who had divided Korea along the 38th parallel and who now headed the State Department's Far Eastern desk, reported there was "no evidence of war brewing"[46] in that country. Yet just five days after Rusk's optimistic assessment, North Korea invaded South Korea, a surprise that shocked the world as much as the Japanese attack on Pearl Harbor had nine years earlier.

Perhaps the most surprised person on that rainy morning of June 25, 1950, was Capt. Joseph R. Darrigo, a U.S. military adviser stationed on the 38th parallel at Kaesong, just forty miles northwest of the capital of Seoul. The sleeping Darrigo was awakened about daybreak by artillery shell fragments striking his home. The thirty-year-old officer hurriedly dressed and drove his jeep to the center of town, where he was stunned to see soldiers of the North Korean People's Army (NKPA) hopping off a train that had just pulled into the station.

The invaders soon spotted the American and began shooting at him. "Once they'd fired four or five bullets and I still hadn't been hit, I figured God was steering them away from me,"[47] Darrigo commented years later. Darrigo then sped away to the nearby headquarters of the Republic of Korea (ROK) First Division, the unit he was advising. The Korean War had begun.

SHOULD IT HAVE BEEN A SURPRISE?

This invasion by ninety thousand NKPA soldiers, however, should not have surprised officials of South Korea or its protector, the United States. Historian Stanley Sandler writes that U.S. intelligence reports had often predicted the possibility of such an attack:

> Although it is generally believed that General [Douglas] MacArthur's Intelligence Section did not anticipate an invasion from the North, this is not the case. Far East Command G-2 (Intelligence) as early as December, 1949 reported that [North Korea] had set March or April of 1950 for its D-Day, and progressively warned in the intervening months that the military buildup in the north had to be for offensive purposes. . . . One report in March even predicted an attack in June 1950 but was ignored by MacArthur.[48]

NORTH KOREA SURPRISES THE WORLD ■ 37

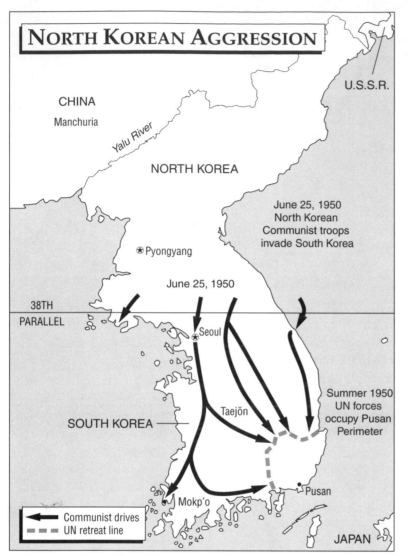

NORTH KOREAN AGGRESSION

CHINA

Manchuria

Yalu River

U.S.S.R.

NORTH KOREA

⊛ Pyongyang

June 25, 1950
North Korean
Communist troops
invade South Korea

June 25, 1950

38TH
PARALLEL

⊛ Seoul

SOUTH KOREA

Taejŏn

Summer 1950
UN forces
occupy Pusan
Perimeter

Mokp'o

• Pusan

◄■■■ Communist drives
- - - UN retreat line

JAPAN

tilities were so intense in October 1949 that veteran journalist A. T. Steele wrote, "An unadmitted shooting war between the governments of the U.S. and Russia [through their Korean allies] is in effect today along the 38th parallel."[49]

Similar border incidents had occurred off and on since 1946, consisting of major raids and military probes across the 38th parallel by soldiers of both Koreas. In the fall of 1949, South Korean president Syngman Rhee, who was often the aggressor in the clashes, brashly told an American journalist, "I am sure that we could take Pyongyang [North Korea's capital] . . . in three days."[50]

U.S. officials were also caught off guard by the invasion due to their preoccupation with Europe and their expectation that a shooting war would first erupt there, not in Asia. As Korean War historian Stanley Sandler notes, "America's enduring foreign policy focus [during the Cold War] would remain that of Western Europe."[51]

Even the ROK army units defending the 38th parallel were unprepared because they did not expect a major attack. Only a third of the thirty-eight thousand soldiers assigned to guard the border were man-

MacArthur, who commanded all U.S. troops in the Pacific and was also governing occupied Japan, and other officials had disregarded the warnings because U.S. and South Korean intelligence agencies had inaccurately predicted nonexistent invasions many times in the past. War had also seemed much more likely a year earlier, when a series of border clashes between North and South raged between May and December. The hos-

ning their posts, another third were on leave helping their families harvest soybeans and rice, and the remainder were in reserve locations ten to thirty miles behind the main defensive positions.

Thus the South Koreans were heavily outnumbered when North Korean soldiers stormed across the border. The better-armed NKPA sent ROK units reeling backward, quickly captured Seoul, and soon appeared ready to overrun all of South Korea.

AMERICA'S RESPONSE

Americans first learned of the attack in a story filed by United Press (UP), a wire ser-vice that provided news from around the world. The report arrived in Washington Saturday night, June 24 (Korea time is thirteen hours ahead of America's east coast time), beating by several hours the formal announcement of hostilities from John J. Muccio, the U.S. ambassador in South Korea.

Alerted to the invasion at 9:04 P.M. by a UP reporter calling for reaction to the hostilities, Secretary of State Dean Acheson immediately telephoned President Harry S. Truman, who was at his home in Independence, Missouri. Stunned and angered by the attack, Truman's immediate reaction was that the United States had to meet the Communist challenge. "Dean," Truman said, "we've got to stop [them] no matter what."[52]

Two North Korean soldiers cut away a barbed wire fence during the invasion of South Korea.

At the time the president, as did everyone else around the world, believed North Korea had acted on orders from Soviet premier Joseph Stalin. But in the decades since, the release of classified papers and other documents have shown that North Korean premier Kim Il Sung originated the attack, traveling to Moscow near the end of 1949 to seek Stalin's permission to invade South Korea. Stalin turned Kim down several times before finally granting him permission in April 1950. The Soviet Union provided some military support and helped draw up the invasion plan, which included re-laying railroad track into Kaesong that the North had previously destroyed (one reason Darrigo was so shocked to see enemy soldiers getting off a train the morning the war began).

But Stalin told Kim that North Korea would have to win the war by itself, and before the attack withdrew seven thousand Soviet military advisers, which he hoped would make the United States believe the Soviet Union was not involved in the invasion. "If you get kicked in the teeth," Stalin said, "I shall not lift a finger to help you."[53] When Stalin told Kim that if he needed help he should get it from China's Mao Tsetung, Kim also unveiled his plan to Mao. The Chinese leader reluctantly gave his approval, even though he was worried that a war in Korea could be expanded by the west to include attacks on his own nation.

In the end, though, who ordered the attack actually mattered very little. The problem confronting Truman was what to do about it. He soon decided to appeal to the United Nations (UN) for help in saving South Korea.

THE UN GOES TO WAR

In June 1945, fifty nations met in San Francisco, California, to establish a new global organization called the United Nations (UN) to prevent future wars. The UN was the successor to the League of Nations, an international body created after World War I at the insistence of President Woodrow Wilson. The League had failed to prevent another world war, mainly because the United States had refused to become a member.

Truman asked the UN Security Council to help beleaguered South Korea. The Council voted 9–0 to approve a resolution that demanded "the immediate cessation of hostilities," ordered North Korea "to withdraw forthwith their armed forces to the 38th parallel," and advised its members "to render every assistance to the United Nations in the execution of this resolution and to refrain from giving assistance to the North Korean authorities."[54]

UN Secretary Trygve Lie saw the attack as the first real test of power for the five-year-old peacekeeping organization. "This," Lie said, "is war against the United Nations."[55] Although the war was fought under the authority of the United Nations, the United States provided more than half the manpower and the vast majority of weapons and war matériel. However, soldiers from sixteen other countries including Britain, Turkey, Australia, France, and the Philippines fought in Korea under UN authorization, and eleven more nations provided other forms of assistance.

Truman involved the UN because he believed it was time for the organization to prove it could help keep the peace around

THE UNITED NATIONS IN KOREA

The United Nations (UN) was founded in 1945 in hopes that it could help nations resolve their problems before the disputes got so serious the countries involved would go to war over them. When fighting began in Korea, the UN decided it had to help South Korea. In The Oxford 50th Anniversary Book of the United Nations, *Charles Patterson explains the nature of the UN involvement:*

"The Allied military campaign in the Korean War was more of a joint U.S.–South Korean effort than a United Nations operation. Although the unified command reported to the UN, the United States decided what it reported. Also, the vast bulk of the Allied forces were either American or South Korean."

Although the United States was dominant in making military decisions, the war was waged under the auspices of the United Nations. The rationale for helping Korea is contained in the preamble to the UN Charter, which is quoted in Patterson's book:

"We the peoples of the United Nations, determined to save succeeding generations from the scourge of war, which twice in our lifetime has brought untold sorrow to mankind, and to reaffirm faith in fundamental human rights, in the dignity and worth of the human person, in the equal rights of men and women and of nations large and small, and to establish conditions under which justice and respect for the obligations arising from treaties and other sources of international law can be maintained, and to promote social progress and better standards of life . . . have resolved to combine our efforts to accomplish these aims."

Despite a dominant U.S. presence, the Korean War was fought under the auspices of the United Nations (pictured here).

the world. When the nations of the world had gathered in San Francisco to form the group, Truman told them, "If we do not want to die together in war, we must live together in peace. We must build a new world—a far better world—one in which the eternal dignity of man is respected."[56]

In the Security Council, any one member had the power to veto a proposal by voting against it. The Soviet Union's Security Council representative, Jacob Malik, would certainly have done so had he been at the meeting. He was absent though, as he had been for several months in protest of the UN's refusal to admit Communist China. Malik was also not in attendance late on the night of June 27 when the UN, with a 7–1 vote, approved an even more important resolution. The Security Council recommended that "the Members of the United Nations furnish such assistance to the Republic of Korea as may be necessary to repel the armed attack and to restore international peace and security in the area."[57]

The second part of that recommendation authorized member nations to provide military aid to stop the invasion. But Truman had decided even before the second UN vote was taken to try to save Korea.

TRUMAN ACTS ON HIS OWN

In a meeting the morning of June 27, Truman told congressmen from both parties, "I have ordered United States sea and air forces to give the Korean government troops cover and support."[58] Truman made the decision without seeking the consent of Congress because he believed he had to act immediately to save South Korea. However, the president had still not taken the more significant step of committing U.S. ground troops to the conflict.

When MacArthur flew to Seoul on June 29 to assess the situation, he found the capital city in flames and the South Korean army in full rout. Realizing that South Korea would be conquered in just a few weeks by the advancing Communists, MacArthur advised Defense Department officials of the severity of the situation and concluded, "The only hope of holding the present line [then just south of Seoul] is through the introduction of U.S. ground combat forces into the Korean battle area."[59]

The next day, June 30, Truman approved a request for ground troops from MacArthur and the Joint Chiefs of Staff, the officers who head the four branches of the military: the Army, Navy, Air Force, and Marines. In a meeting later that day when the president revealed his decision to congressional leaders, only Republican Senator Kenneth S. Wherry dared asked Truman why he had not consulted Congress. The president said he had acted quickly because he feared that Congress might delay so long, it would be too late to save Korea.

When the conflict later became unpopular in America it was disparagingly labeled "Truman's War," and he was criticized for not securing congressional approval to commit soldiers to Korea. Congress, the only branch of the government empowered to do so, never issued a formal declaration of war against North Korea.

The president further complicated his situation by always referring to the conflict as a UN "police action," and not a war, in what was a misguided, feeble attempt to downgrade to Americans the seriousness of U.S. involvement in Korea. Regardless, the initial reaction to Truman's decision was positive from congressmen of both parties, newspapers across the country, and the public. Even the man who would succeed him as president, Dwight D. Eisenhower, then still an army general in Europe, said, "We'll have a dozen Koreas soon if we don't take a firm stand."[60]

TASK FORCE SMITH

As Truman was ordering U.S. troops into South Korea, units of the ROK Army were being pushed south relentlessly by the NKPA. Advancing behind the protection of heavy Soviet T-34 tanks, the North Koreans were threatening to capture the entire peninsula.

The first U.S. troops were sent to Korea on July 1 to stop the Communist advance, 406 men from the Twenty-fourth Infantry Division, a unit dispatched from Japan nicknamed Task Force Smith after its top-ranking officer, Lt. Col. (Lieutenant Colonel) Charles Bradley Smith. Their job was to stop the advance so the rest of the Twenty-fourth Division, commanded by Gen. William F. Dean, the First Cavalry, and the Twenty-fifth Infantry Divisions could be deployed. When the two divisons did arrive they were collectively known as the Eighth

After witnessing the desperate situation in South Korea, General Douglas MacArthur (foreground) advised that U.S. combat troops be sent to Korea.

United States Army, Korea (EUSAK) and commanded by Lt. Gen. Walton Harris Walker.

Smith's men were airlifted to the seacoast city of Pusan and traveled by truck and railroad to the city of Taejon. Members of Task Force Smith arrived full of confidence, believing that as soon as the North Koreans realized they were battling Americans, they would become afraid and run away. But their initial encounters would be anything but U.S. triumphs over an awed Asian foe.

Lieutenant Colonel Smith decided to have his men defend an area about three miles north of the town of Osan. They arrived there by truck at 3 A.M. on July 5, and as dawn broke they saw a long line of enemy tanks and soldiers approaching. The fight began shortly after 8 A.M. and by 2:30 P.M. the North Koreans had forced Smith's men to retreat, their delusions of superiority shattered by the NKPA's fighting ability and the Americans' own inferior equipment; U.S. soldiers had no tanks, antitank mines, or armor-piercing bazookas to stop the Soviet tanks.

Smith later admitted that ordering a retreat was a tough decision but the correct one. In the initial U.S. engagement with the enemy, nearly half of Smith's men became casualties, a military term for soldiers who are killed, wounded, captured, too ill to fight on, or declared missing in action. Smith knew that his force had to retreat or it would be destroyed:

> To stand and die, or to try to get the remains of my Task Force out of there? I could last, at best, only another hour, and then lose everything I had. I chose to try to get out, in hopes that we would live to fight another day.[61]

The remnants of Task Force Smith fled in a hurried, unstructured retreat that was the first of many withdrawals American forces would endure in July 1950, one of the worst months in U.S. military history. The retreats were so helter-skelter that even Gen. William Dean was captured while trying to flee the advancing North Koreans. It is rare for such a high-ranking officer to be captured, and Dean spent nearly three years as a prisoner of war.

That first retreat was not only humiliating but degrading as Task Force Smith, in a breach of military tradition, abandoned its wounded. While one of Smith's lieutenants,

Members of Task Force Smith arrive in South Korea.

Heroism At Chochiwon

One of the reasons U.S. soldiers suffered a series of defeats in the early days of the Korean War was that their often old and outdated equipment sometimes failed to work. Despite such problems, Col. Carl Bernard won a Distinguished Service Cross for heroism for his actions on July 11, 1950, in a battle at Chochiwon, a town on the main highway from Seoul to Pusan. He wrote about his experience in the March 8, 1999, issue of Newsweek *magazine:*

"I lost nearly 101 men killed or captured out of a rifle company of 130 people. Thirty-three men died in captivity. When [his unit] got down to fighting tanks, I [realized] our bazookas didn't work. The seat closest to the fire is reserved for the Army officers who knew [the weapons did not work] and didn't tell me. I climbed on the top of the first Soviet-made T-34 tank. The Koreans would open their [door], stick out a burp [machine] gun and fire it to clear people off the tank's back. Being safe on top [of the tank], I hit the plug with my rifle butt and broke the chain. The sergeant with me, Hugh Brown, best fighting man I've ever known, put 15 rounds from his M-1 through the open port when the burp-gunner paused to reload. We got the next tank by pouring a five-gallon can of gas on its hot engine compartment. Then we went back and burned the other tank. We were low on ammunition and couldn't get resupplied. Koreans had already [gotten around] our position and had machine guns on the ridge behind us. My own platoon was destroyed because we stayed too long in a losing fight. I took the DSC [Distinguished Service Cross] citation for the Chochiwon fight back to [his unit's] location. My handwritten note said [the medal] was for the men who were killed or captured there."

badly wounded himself, was dragging himself past six injured men who were unable even to crawl away, one of them asked what would happen to those left behind. The lieutenant passed him a hand grenade, saying, "This is the best I can do for you."[62]

The rout was the first of a series of disastrous defeats as the invaders pushed South Korean and U.S. forces down the Korean peninsula until they finally managed to regroup and establish a defensive perimeter near Pusan. There, they would make a final stand against the advancing NKPA.

Unprepared U.S. Troops

Americans were in shock that the vaunted U.S. Army had wilted before the North Koreans. The reality was that besides being heavily outnumbered, they had experienced severe equipment problems and were not prepared for war. Many of their supplies were old and worn out, most radios failed to work, and many of their weapons, from M-1 rifles to mortars, were not fit for combat. One officer, for example, had to raid a schoolhouse south of Osan and rip a map of Korea out of a geography book because he had no map of the country he was trying to defend.

Even worse, the soldiers themselves, accustomed to easy duty in American-occupied Japan, were not mentally or emotionally ready for combat. Colonel Roy E. Appleman, a historian and veteran of the early fighting, claims:

> A basic fact is that the occupation divisions were not trained, equipped or ready for battle. The great majority of the enlisted men were young and not really interested in being soldiers. The recruiting posters that had induced most of these men to enter the Army mentioned all conceivable advantages and promised many good things, but never suggested that the principal business of an army is to fight.[63]

Untested in combat, the young Americans became terrified of the brutal, unconventional North Korean tactics. When the NKPA broke through their lines, U.S. soldiers would often flee in uncontrollable panic instead of in a measured, orderly retreat. The emotional frenzy that led to this breakdown in discipline was termed "bug out fever," a condition Stanley Weintraub describes in *MacArthur's War: Korea and the Undoing of an American Hero*:

> "Bugout fever" in the first weeks of the war was often as irrational as the word

fever implied. It was also a response to North Korean tactics, which were to follow frontal assaults with flanking attacks, cutting off units and forcing surrenders, then murdering most captives after binding their wrists behind them. Recognizing what could happen to them even if they were not killed in action, soldiers often withdrew in a suicidal hurry, abandoning gear that would slow their retreat.[64]

The most notorious "bugout" unit was the Twenty-fourth Infantry Division, whose soldiers fled for their lives from a battle on July 29 near Sangju, leaving behind machine guns, mortars, rocket launchers, and wounded buddies. Their conduct in that and other battles early in the war earned the Twenty-fourth a reputation it was never able to live down. Other soldiers composed a song called the "Bugout Boogie," which included the following lyrics:

> When the Commie mortars start to chug,
>
> The ol' Deuce Four begins to bug.
>
> When you hear the pitter-patter of little feet,
>
> It's the ol' Deuce Four in full retreat.[65]

THE PUSAN LINE

In late July, Lt. General Walker met with MacArthur in Korea, and they decided that the only way to stop the advancing NKPA was to pull their forces back even further, regroup, and defend a line north of Pusan along the Naktong River, which they believed would be an easy position to hold.

U.S. troops retreat to Pusan, where MacArthur hoped to regroup and stop the North Korean advance.

On July 29, Walker assembled the high-ranking officers who would organize the defensive line and told them the new position had to be held at all costs:

> We are fighting a battle against time. There will be no more retreating, withdrawal or readjustment of the lines or any other term you choose. There is no line behind us to which we can retreat. Every unit must counterattack to keep the enemy in a state of confusion. . . . A retreat to Pusan would be one of the greatest butcheries in history. We must fight until the end. Capture by these people is worse than death itself. We will fight as a team. If some of us die, we will die fighting together.[66]

In military terms, it was a "stand or die" order. It meant no more running, no more retreating—with the sea now at their backs, there was simply nowhere else to go. On August 1, elements of the U.S. Eighth Army and ROK troops began to establish the new defensive position along the Naktong River. The Pusan Perimeter was a fortified defensive line that formed an upright rectangle about 100 miles tall and 50 miles wide; it was bordered by the Naktong on most of its left (or west) side and the Sea of Japan on its right, with rugged mountains to the north and the Korea Strait to the south.

In early August the North Koreans attacked the Pusan Perimeter with ten divisions. The fighting was fierce throughout August and September in engagements like the Battle of the Naktong Bulge (August 5–19), in which the North Koreans attempted to cross the river three times. A series of Pusan Perimeter clashes took place from August 27 to September 15 in some of the heaviest fighting of the war, but the combined ROK and U.S. forces successfully held the line.

One reason for this success was that more U.S. troops had arrived, and by August 29 Scottish and English troops had joined them, creating a true UN army and increasing combined Allied strength to ninety-two thousand men, a greater force than the attacking NKPA. A second major factor was U.S. airpower; bombers disrupted North Korean supply lines and attacked ground troops with devastating results.

AN ALLIED SURPRISE

When it became apparent that the Pusan Perimeter would hold, MacArthur began to plan a counterattack. In a bold, daring move, he decided to land U.S. forces behind the advancing North Koreans at Inchon, a port on Korea's western coast. It was a risky gamble, but one that would dramatically reverse the tide of war.

4 Victory at Inchon, Disaster When China Enters the War

When the Korean War began, Gen. Douglas MacArthur, a hero for leading Allied forces to victory in World War II, already held a host of impressive titles including Supreme Commander of the Allied Powers in occupied Japan, where he ruled the shattered nation with an iron hand. On July 7, 1950, when the United Nations approved forming a unified army, he received another weighty designation—commander of UN forces trying to save South Korea.

President Harry S. Truman, however, always thought of MacArthur as the "supreme egotist" because he believed the brilliant military commander considered himself "something of a god."[67] Yet it was just this unbecoming quality of arrogant self-confidence that allowed MacArthur to devise a daring, ingenious plan that would result in a series of spectacular victories over North Korea. "We shall land at [the port city of] Inchon and I shall crush them,"[68] MacArthur said on August 23 at his Tokyo headquarters.

It was not the first time MacArthur had used that personal pronoun to predict victory. When he arrived in Australia on March 11, 1942, after fleeing from Corregidor, an island in the Philippines, to evade capture by the advancing Japanese during World War II, he had pompously remarked, "I came through, and I shall return."[69] The Office of War Information suggested he change the quote to the more humble "We shall return" before releasing it to the news media, but MacArthur refused. And when the general waded ashore on the Philippine island of Leyte in October 1944 after U.S. forces had landed on it, he announced, "I have returned."[70] The quote, one of the most famous in military history, underscores his unwillingness to share the glory of his accomplishment with the soldiers who fought and died to make it happen.

On August twenty-third, MacArthur met with other top military officials and spent forty-five minutes defending his plan to land at Inchon, a port city on Korea's west coast far behind enemy lines, as part of a wider strategy to cut the North Korean People's Army (NKPA) in half and win back the capital city of Seoul, only twenty miles away from Inchon. Although even MacArthur admitted that it appeared to be a big gamble, he claimed it would succeed, "for the enemy commander will reason that no one would be so brash as to

General MacArthur (left) with South Korean president Syngman Rhee.

make such an attempt. Surprise is the most vital element for success in war."[71]

Yet it was also MacArthur's arrogance that would later blind him to the possibility of China's entry into the fighting. And that miscalculation would be the most fatal of the Korean War.

OPERATION CHROMITE

In World War II, MacArthur's winning strategy had included daring amphibious landings to secure territory behind enemy lines in the Southwest Pacific as he bypassed Japanese strongholds in an attempt to isolate their forces. He proposed this same tactic to capture Inchon, even though

other top military leaders considered his plan risky. "We drew up a list of every conceivable natural and geographic handicap [to the U.S. invasion], and Inchon had 'em all,"[72] admitted Lt. Cmdr. Arlie Capps.

The U.S. military was familiar with Inchon; it was where American soldiers first landed in September 1945 to begin their occupation of Korea. Military leaders understood that to reach Inchon, warships and troop transports would have to advance along a narrow ten-mile waterway called the Flying Fish Channel, which was shallow and at low tide had large mudflats. The harbor entrance was also guarded by Wolmido (Moon Tip) Island, and from its hills enemy artillery could shell U.S. vessels. If just one ship was seriously damaged or became stranded on the mudflats, it could obstruct the channel and doom the landing.

When representatives of the Joint Chiefs of Staff (JCS) and other top officers met with MacArthur, they asked him to scrap the plan because so many things could go wrong. But he overcame their objections with a dramatic defense of what would be called Operation Chromite. MacArthur argued:

> By seizing Seoul [after taking Inchon] I would completely paralyze the enemy's supply system. Without munitions and food they will soon be helpless and disorganized and can easily be overpowered. I can almost hear the ticking of the second hand of destiny. We must act now or we will die.[73]

Five days later, the JCS and President Truman gave MacArthur their grudging approval. Planning for the Inchon landing began in September 1950.

THE INCHON LANDING

Fears that Inchon could turn into a disaster seemed to be coming true in early September when two typhoons struck Japan and Korea, endangering preparations for Operation Chromite. But when the time came to act, everything went as planned. On September 13, two U.S. and two British cruisers and six U.S. destroyers made their way up the Flying Fish Channel and shelled Wolmi-do and Inchon, a process repeated the next day to weaken enemy defenses. Allied ships had already been attacking the

---

WAS THE INCHON LANDING NECESSARY?

Most historians consider the amphibious landing at Inchon to be Gen. Douglas MacArthur's finest hour. In an article in Military Review *forty-five years after it took place, Wilson A. Heefner, a retired Army colonel who served in Korea, assessed Operation Chromite. He praised the planning and execution of the landing but, as have many historians, questioned whether it was necessary:*

"Having critically examined multiple accounts of the Inchon amphibious operation and having actually walked the terrain of the Wolmi-do and Inchon beachheads, I conclude that the Inchon invasion must be ranked as one of the most audacious [bold] and successful amphibious operations of all time. Whether, as MacArthur contended, the invasion was necessary to save Eighth Army from destruction in the Pusan Perimeter must, however, be seriously questioned. My studies lead me to believe that the [North Korean People's Army] at this point was weak, its long logistic lines having been interdicted by uncontested U.S. air power. I have no doubt that [Eighth Army Lt. Gen. Walton Harris] Walker was acquiring limited strength that would have enabled him to break out of the perimeter, possibly by the end of September. But undoubtedly the Inchon invasion, threatening to cut completely the logistic lines and route of escape for the NKPA, accelerated the collapse of the enemy. [Claims by some military experts] that the risks of the operation outweighed any possible gains has questionable merit, for Inchon did hasten the liberation of South Korea and the almost complete destruction of the NKPA as an effective fighting force, saving thousands of American and South Korean lives. Thus, the operation stands as a tremendous tactical success, but the overall strategic implications for the ultimate outcome of the Korean War were much less auspicious [favorable]."

---

defenses for several weeks, but the new bombardment was much more intense.

The plan's biggest risk was the short time available to accomplish the landing in the shallow sea channel, which was navigable only at high tide. The first high tide would peak at 6:59 A.M., but within two hours it would recede and strand UN forces until reinforcements could arrive on the next high tide at 7:19 P.M. MacArthur had assembled more than 250 ships and transports to land 80,000 soldiers, and at 6:33 A.M. on September 15 the landing began.

To MacArthur's delight, and the even greater relief of his soldiers, Operation Chromite worked perfectly. UN forces generally met little resistance from the cowed North Koreans and by 11 A.M. had captured Inchon with only 174 U.S. casualties, including 21 deaths. In *America in the Korean War*, Edward F. Dolan describes how U.S. Marines raced up a hill from the beach of Wolmi-do:

> As the men of one unit moved up its slopes, North Korean soldiers suddenly appeared in front of them, climbing out of foxholes and holding their hands high in surrender. Survivors of the vicious bombardments of the past days, they were exhausted, dazed, and afraid they were going to be killed. They sighed with relief when the Marines sent them back down to the beach under guard.[74]

The landing succeeded because it surprised the North Koreans and because heavy shelling neutralized their defenses. Later that day, in uncharacteristically humble language, MacArthur filed his initial report to the JCS: "Our losses are light. . . . The command distinguished itself. The whole operation is proceeding on schedule."[75]

RECAPTURING SOUTH KOREA

This brilliant maneuver far north of the main battlefront became the catalyst for a decisive turnaround. In the next few weeks UN forces disrupted NKPA supply lines and divided their armies, ejected the invaders from the south, and captured more than 125,000 prisoners.

The first objective was to free nearby Seoul. Allied soldiers fought their way to the capital and only two days after landing at Inchon began a battle that would rage for more than a week. The fighting was fierce as they met intense opposition from North Korean soldiers, and they had to battle through streets made nearly impassable by rubble from artillery bombardments and air assaults. Seoul was secured on September 26, and three days later MacArthur and South Korean president Syngman Rhee held a victory ceremony in the bombed-out National Assembly Hall.

The death and devastation that returning U.S. diplomats saw in the ruins of Seoul sickened them, but MacArthur, believing he had won the war, was in a jaunty mood, and Rhee lavishly praised him, saying, "We love you as the savior of our race."[76] The liberation of South Korea, however, had been costly. By September 29, U.S. casualties in the war numbered more than 27,000, including 6,000 dead, 19,000 wounded, and 2,500 captured or missing in action.

Within two weeks of the Inchon landing (left) U.S. forces had driven the North Korean army across the 38th parallel and captured more than 125,000 prisoners (below).

CROSSING THE 38TH PARALLEL

When the Allied victories sent NKPA soldiers scurrying back north across the border, the United States and United Nations faced a difficult decision: Should they pursue the enemy across the 38th parallel? The June 27 UN resolution authorized forces only "to repel the armed attack and to restore international peace and security in the area,"[77] but U.S. and UN officials now began to debate whether the mission should be changed to conquering North Korea and reuniting the nation.

Grave risks were involved in crossing into North Korea, including the possibility that the Soviet Union or China could enter the war. But the euphoria over a series of stunning victories after so many terrible defeats combined with the pleas of Rhee, who held out hopes of forming a democratic,

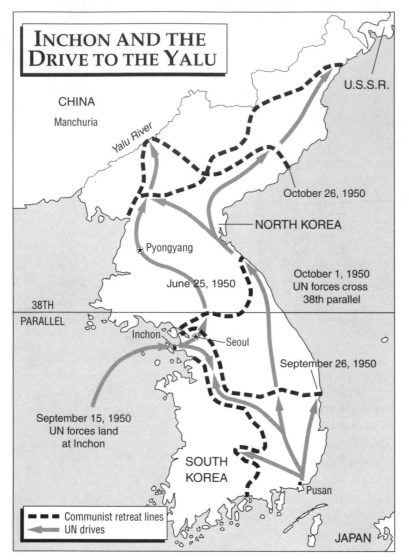

INCHON AND THE DRIVE TO THE YALU

CHINA

Manchuria

Yalu River

U.S.S.R.

October 26, 1950

NORTH KOREA

Pyongyang

October 1, 1950
UN forces cross
38th parallel

June 25, 1950

38TH
PARALLEL

Inchon

Seoul

September 26, 1950

September 15, 1950
UN forces land
at Inchon

SOUTH
KOREA

Pusan

- - - Communist retreat lines
→ UN drives

JAPAN

provinces bordering the Soviet Union or in the area along the [Chinese] border."[78] The JCS and Truman did not want to create any border incidents that would provoke China or the Soviet Union. MacArthur responded on September 30 with a message that seemed to accept the order but ended with the contrary statement, "I regard all of Korea open for our military operations."[79] Although MacArthur had bluntly stated his intention to do what he wanted, no matter how the order read, the JCS and Truman accepted his response and did not ask him to clarify what he meant. It was a mistake on their part that would prove fatal to the course of the war.

UN troops first crossed the 38th parallel on October 1 and a full-scale invasion northward began eight days later. UN forces rolled to victory after victory over

unified Korea, led Truman to decide to allow MacArthur to cross the 38th parallel. On September 27, the Joint Chiefs of Staff ordered MacArthur to enter North Korea and destroy its armed forces, a mission the UN General Assembly would concur with in a resolution it passed on October 7.

The Joint Chiefs, however, stipulated that "as a matter of policy, no non-Korean ground forces will be used in the [country's] northeast

the shattered NKPA and by October 19 had captured Pyongyang, the North Korean capital. MacArthur, in another of his frequent but brief visits to war zones, triumphantly visited Pyongyang. Landing at the airfield, he joked, "Any celebrities to greet me? Where's Kim Buck Tooth?"[80] a reference to the elusive Premier Kim Il Sung that was a variation on a racial slur dating back to World War II. Kim was not there, but Red Chinese troops were already secretly infiltrating North Korea and would soon be ready for battle.

IGNORING CHINESE WARNINGS

Mao Tse-tung had watched with dismay as the North Koreans were defeated and expelled from South Korea. When UN forces in late September decided to invade North Korea, he became fearful they would not stop at the Yalu River, the border between the two countries, but instead carry the war into China in an extended attack against Communism. Fearing this possibility, Chinese officials had issued several warnings that U.S. officials failed to heed.

In his October 1 speech on the first anniversary of the establishment of Communist China, Premier Chou En-lai warned the west that China "will not tolerate foreign aggression and will not stand aside should the imperialists wantonly invade the territory of their neighbor [North Korea]."[81] Then Chou on October 3 issued a more direct threat, saying, "The South Koreans did not matter, but American intrusion into North Korea would encounter Chinese resistance."[82] In other words, it was all right for South Koreans to invade North Korea, but not UN forces. U.S. officials received the message, but Secretary of State Dean Acheson dismissed it as a bluff intended to stop the invasion.

With victory appearing certain, President Truman flew halfway around the world to

President Harry S. Truman (left) meets with General MacArthur on Wake Island, October 15, 1950.

confer with MacArthur on October 15 at Wake Island, an island in the North Pacific that belongs to the United States. In the first meeting ever between the two historic figures, Truman asked MacArthur if China might intercede in the war. "We are no longer fearful of intervention," the general said. "Now that we have bases for our Air Force in Korea, if the Chinese tried to get down to Pyongyang there would be the greatest slaughter."[83] MacArthur was wrong, but he was only passing on reports from intelligence sources, including the fledgling Central Intelligence Agency (CIA), which claimed "the Chinese Communists undoubtedly fear the consequences of war with the United States."[84]

U.S. officials had simply refused to believe Chou's warnings, but the day before the Wake Island conference, Chinese troops had already begun crossing the Yalu River. In the next few weeks 300,000 more would enter North Korea undetected. Fearful of being invaded itself, China had entered the war.

CHINA GOES TO WAR

The Chinese were experts at moving large armies in great secrecy. Their troops traveled on foot, which meant that they had no motor vehicles for enemy reconnaissance to spot from the air. It also meant that the Chinese did not have to stick to roads. They moved only at night, wore clothing over their uniforms that made them resemble refugees if they were sighted, and had white coats that blended in with the snow blanketing the mountainous north-

ern area, making them nearly invisible from the air.

As UN forces advanced north from Pyongyang, Chinese armies commanded by P'eng Teh-huai moved south. They first met on October 25 about fifty miles south of the Chinese border, when a battalion of the Republic of Korea (ROK) Sixth Division marched northwest from the tiny village of Onjong. Running into a large contingent of Chinese, the battalion was beaten back and almost half of its 750 men were killed, wounded, or captured. Another ROK battalion coming up behind them was also attacked but managed to capture two enemy soldiers who, to their great surprise and dismay, were Chinese.

On October 29, ROK troops deserted the front lines after being mauled by Communist troops, and on November 1 the Chinese attacked in force near Unsan, unleashing a general offensive powered by massive numbers of soldiers no one had known were present just a few days earlier. At first, top U.S. officers including Charles A. Willoughby, MacArthur's intelligence chief, refused to believe battlefield reports that Chinese soldiers were present.

Jack Chiles, who worked at MacArthur's Tokyo headquarters, claims that Willoughby was negligent in performing his job: "MacArthur did not want the Chinese to enter the war in Korea. Anything MacArthur wanted, Willoughby produced intelligence for. . . . In this case, Willoughby falsified the intelligence reports [about the early Chinese contacts]. . . . He should have gone to jail."[85] By November 6, though, the Communist offensive was so widespread that even MacArthur had to concede that he

CHAIRMAN MAO'S MASTER STRATEGY

When Gen. Douglas MacArthur ordered UN forces to begin a new offensive on November 25, 1950, he sent his men into a trap set by Chinese chairman Mao Tse-tung. One reason the Communists prevailed over Nationalist leader Chiang Kai-shek in the battle for China is that Mao was a more able military commander. Mao, who had also successfully battled the invading Japanese, outsmarted MacArthur by fooling him in November with a false retreat. In his book In Mortal Combat, *John Toland explains how Mao worked out the plan:*

"Chairman Mao was planning the final steps of his trap in an ancient one-story structure just outside the walls of the Forbidden City [in the Chinese capital of Peking (now Beijing)]. This modest office was where he had lived and worked in seclusion since China's entry into the war. . . . Mao would spend hours, half-sitting, half-lying on his bed, studying ancient Chinese history. He had never attended a military school and was a self-made tactical genius. Through the years he had learned from his own successes and failures. . . . The strategy was simple. The Chinese would open the door, as if retreating. . . . When Mao learned that MacArthur had taken the bait by ordering a general offensive on November 24, he telegraphed [his armies] to launch their own counteroffensive at twilight of the 25th."

---

was facing a new, much more powerful foe. In a communiqué to Washington, he stated:

> While the North Korean Forces with which we were initially engaged have been destroyed or rendered impotent for military action, a new and fresh army faces us, backed up by . . . large alien reserves and adequate supplies within easy reach of the enemy but beyond the limits of our present sphere of military action.[86]

Strangely, however, the Chinese, who were pushing MacArthur's troops back along a wide front, suddenly disappeared. The question was: Why?

A CHINESE PUZZLE

Mao had mysteriously ordered his troops to quit fighting. Given a breathing spell to reassess the situation, MacArthur and his officers mistakenly concluded that the Chinese had fought themselves out and were in retreat. As a result, MacArthur decided to spring a new offensive that he believed could win the war within a few weeks.

On November 24, a day after frontline troops enjoyed a Thanksgiving Day feast that included shrimp cocktail and roast turkey, MacArthur flew to Eighth Army headquarters at Sinanju on the Chongchon River. Announcing the start of a new offensive to clear North Korea of all enemy

U.S. troops at the front enjoy a Thanksgiving meal. Confident that the Americans had beaten the Chinese, MacArthur promised that U.S. forces would be home for Christmas.

soldiers, he commented, "If this operation is successful, I hope we can get the boys home for Christmas."[87]

When reporters relayed his startling prediction around the world, American newspapers nicknamed the new drive the "Home by Christmas Offensive." The military operation began that same day, but soldiers of the Eighth Army and the Marines' X Corps encountered a surprising reality when they ran up against 300,000 Chinese troops. What was even worse than being outnumbered by more than 53,000 soldiers

was the fact that MacArthur had foolishly split his forces, sending the Eighth Army up the east side of North Korea and X Corps up the west. The Chinese had blindly infiltrated between them and on the night of November 25 began attacking from all sides. Historian John Toland explains how Mao, a brilliant military strategist as well as China's political leader, had devised a deadly trap for MacArthur:

> In Peking, Mao [in late November] was in high spirits. His analysis of MacArthur had been correct. Over-

weening self-confidence was luring the supreme commander into a trap. . . . By suddenly withdrawing, Mao guessed that MacArthur, assuming *he* had beaten the Chinese, would push his troops further north. . . . Then the [Chinese] and North Koreans would come out of their hiding places in the wooded mountains and win the decisive battle.[88]

The attacks shocked and terrified UN forces, not only because huge numbers of Chinese kept advancing despite suffering high numbers of casualties from withering defensive fire, but because of the way they fought. War historian Edward F. Dolan describes those first assaults:

> They would come eerily in the night, wave after wave of massed humanity, blowing bugles, horns, and whistles (their signaling system) and shooting flares. Their dead would pile up three deep, and still they would come. But it was not just a question of numbers. The clever ambushes, envelopments, and roadblocks . . . destroyed South Korean regiments and forced the battered Americans to retreat south across the Chongchon River.[89]

Instead of heading home by Christmas, UN forces by that date were being pushed back below the 38th parallel in the longest retreat in U.S. military history. By December 1 the Eighth Army was backpedaling from the Chongchon River in the west, and by December 11, after fierce fighting at the Chosin Reservoir in the east, U.S. Marines of the X Corps were also retreating. On January 5, 1951, the Chinese captured Seoul, the third time the South Korean capital had

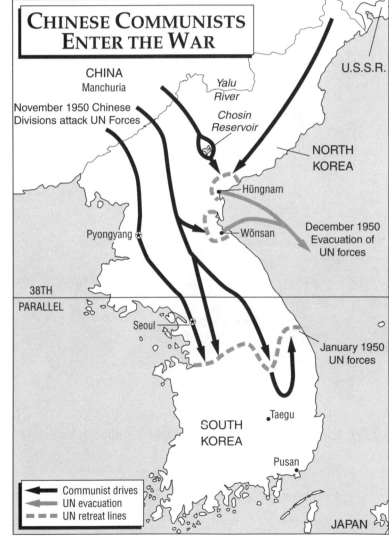

CHINESE COMMUNISTS ENTER THE WAR

CHINA
Manchuria

November 1950 Chinese Divisions attack UN Forces

Yalu River

Chosin Reservoir

U.S.S.R.

NORTH KOREA

Hüngnam

Pyongyang

Wŏnsan

December 1950 Evacuation of UN forces

38TH PARALLEL

Seoul

January 1950 UN forces

Taegu

SOUTH KOREA

Pusan

Communist drives
UN evacuation
UN retreat lines

JAPAN

THE COLD BECOMES AN ENEMY

The bitter conditions of a Korean winter became a second terrible enemy UN forces had to contend with during the war. U.S. soldiers first encountered it in late November 1950, when they were sent reeling back across the 38th parallel by the Communist Chinese. In Korea: The Untold Story of the War, *Joseph C. Goulden discusses how the cold affected soldiers as they retreated from the Chosin Reservoir in South Korea:*

"When they tried to describe the cold later—be it to a war correspondent the next week, in a letter home the next month, in an interview three decades later—the Marines, to a man, had to grope for words. 'It was impossible,' said one former sergeant, 'to wear enough clothes to keep warm, much less comfortable. You were bundled so heavily, what with the gloves and the parka and the long john underwear and the hoods and what all, that you were bound to generate some body sweat. What happened, the minute you stopped moving around, it would turn to ice, right inside your damned clothes. Ever touch a piece of cold metal out of doors on a winter morning? Well, imagine trying to keep friendly with an M-one or a carbine. That steel was ice. Put bare flesh on it, and you stuck, and the only way to get loose was to lose some skin. One time my *mouth* literally froze shut, my spittle mixed up with my whiskers.'"

The harsh, cold Korean winter soon became the second enemy of U.S. troops.

changed hands since the war began. Even more dispiriting, on December 23, Eighth Army general Walton H. Walker was killed when a truck collided with his jeep. UN forces were in disarray before the onrushing Red Chinese.

Even in retreat, however, U.S. soldiers at times managed to acquit themselves well against two terrible foes—the Communists and the inhuman cold of a Korean winter, which froze their food, medicine, and weapons as well as their bodies. Military historian Robert Leckie writes in *The Wars of America* that the First Marine and Seventh Army Divisions were especially valiant in withdrawing from the Chosin River from November 27 to December 11:

> The fragmented units drew together, fighting from town to town, swelling in strength and ardor, until at last they broke out of the trap in what was beyond question the greatest fighting withdrawal in the history of modern arms.[90]

American soldiers battled so bravely around "Frozen Chosin," their nickname for the reservoir, that they were awarded seventeen Medals of Honor and seventy Navy Crosses. Allied troops killed or wounded more than 40,000 Chinese while suffering only 7,500 casualties themselves, more than half of them from frostbite due to wind-chill temperatures that plummeted to seventy-five degrees below zero.

MacArthur's Gamble Fails

In just a few months MacArthur had been responsible for both sublime victory and disastrous defeat. But even though his miscalculations had proven fatal, he was still revered by his men, as shown by a letter Lt. Col. James H. Polk wrote to his wife from Tokyo:

> The whole of [the general's staff] . . . has a bad case of the blues. . . . The old man, MacA, I mean, is really one hell of a gambler. . . . Well, this time he gambled it a little too hard and really pressed his luck a bit too far and the whole house fell in on him. He had chanced staking it all on one big throw, and for once the great MacA's luck ran out on him. He just didn't believe that the whole [Chinese army] would be thrown against him. I really admired him in defeat, but it sorta looks like the end of an era.[91]

It was. Within a few months Truman would recall MacArthur for insubordination. But the great general would be a casualty not only of his own military miscues, but the political infighting raging at home over a war that was swiftly becoming unpopular.

5 The Korean War Divides America

When President Harry S. Truman almost single-handedly decided the United States had to defend South Korea, his fellow countrymen supported him. A nation that since the end of World War II had become increasingly jittery about a war with Communists appeared relieved that the wait was over; America had finally taken up arms to stop the Soviet Union—which it mistakenly believed had ordered the attack—from conquering the rest of the world. After the president decided to help South Korea, *Christian Science Monitor* reporter Joseph C. Harsch wrote:

> I have lived and worked in and out of [Washington, D.C.] for 20 years. Never before in that time have I felt such a sense of relief and unity pass through this city. Mr. Truman obviously did much more than he was expected to do, and almost exactly what most individuals seemed to wish he would do.[92]

Yet during the first year of fighting, the unanimity that greeted Truman's bold decision slowly died, a victim of displeasure over defeats, anger over the war's accompanying sacrifices, especially deaths and injuries to loved ones who were fighting, and a growing despondency that this was a war the United States could not win. Americans who had willingly made huge personal sacrifices, both on the battlefield and at home, to win World Wars I and II became divided about their nation's participation in the conflict. In *The Wars of America*, Robert Leckie comments:

> At home, the American public was not so much shamed by newspaper accounts [of defeats], which very often exaggerated GI shortcomings, as angered by them. The people do not ask, "Why did they run?" but "Why are they there?" The answer to the last question was never convincing to Americans. . . . The Korean War did not appear to be what it actually was, the application of the Truman Doctrine to Asia, but rather seemed an alien conflict. It looked more like a war fought in Asia to save one Asian nation from another, and as such it was "none of our business."[93]

UNPREPARED FOR WAR

Although Americans in June 1950 were as ready for war as their president, they soon discovered that the United States was woefully unprepared for combat. Historian John Toland explains:

> Harry Truman's decision was courageous but could not have come at a worse time. The state of the U.S. military was deplorable, partially because of Truman's dislike of spending public money and his contempt for generals and admirals. Despite his own tough, Cold War policy of containing Communism, he had already cut the [defense] budget by one third. Instead, money was being spent on foreign aid to nations opressed by the Soviets.[94]

At the end of World War II there were 12 million men and women in the service, but the nation quickly began dismantling the world's most powerful armed forces because Americans wanted their loved ones brought back home. In *The Wars of America*, Robert Leckie writes, "America wanted to disarm and get back to normal. Even though the Red Army was occupying half of Europe, the cry was bring the boys home."[95] The armed forces were cut to 3 million by 1948, a figure that was halved again by the start of the Korean War.

Another reason for reducing the size of the military was that many leaders believed the atomic bomb had made the nation so

U.S. soldiers celebrate after being discharged at the end of World War II. Deep cuts in the military's budget left the United States unprepared for combat when the Korean War began five years later.

powerful it would never have to go to war again; the mere threat of another Hiroshima would scare countries so much they would never dare challenge America. But historian Joseph C. Goulden writes, "Korea shattered the American illusion that atomic weaponry had outmoded the foot soldier."[96] The United States discovered that even though it had the atomic bomb, some nations were still willing to risk war to get what they wanted.

When a series of crushing early defeats highlighted its weakness, America began to rearm itself. Truman on July 10 sought an emergency appropriation of $10 billion, but Congress gave him $11.6 billion, nearly as much as the $13 billion defense budget for the entire fiscal year. Noted *Time* magazine: "Republicans were tripping over Democrats in their eagerness to give President Truman what he thought he needed to win in Korea and prepare for the next Korea, whenever or wherever it might turn out to be."[97]

Congress eventually voted $48.2 billion for defense in fiscal 1950–51 and $60 billion the next year. Thus began an arms race between the United States and Soviet Union that would last for four decades and eventually weaken the economies of both nations. The two sides would spend hundreds of billions of dollars to strengthen their armies and create more powerful bombs and missile systems that could deliver nuclear warheads anywhere in the world.

Congress also extended the Selective Service Act for one year and authorized Truman to order National Guard and Reserve units into active duty, and the Defense Department hired 230,000 civilians to free soldiers for combat. Although an August Gallup Poll showed that two-thirds of Americans supported intervention, many of those called up for duty were angry; most had fought in World War II and believed they had fulfilled their duty to their country. Despite their misgivings they were needed again, this time to fight Communism.

NUCLEAR FEARS

In the post–World War II era the new Red Scare that had swept the nation caused by a fear of Communism was now heightened by anxiety over a possible nuclear attack by the Soviets, creating a frightened mood verging on panic. These worries in the early fifties led Americans to do things that seem crazy today.

In January 1951, television cameras—themselves new in that era—were on hand as Mrs. Ruth Colhoun, a Los Angeles, California, mother of three, broke ground for a backyard bomb shelter. She exclaimed that the shelter would have practical uses besides protecting her family. "It will make a wonderful place for the children to play in and it will be a good storehouse, too," she said. "I do a lot of canning and bottling in the summer, you know."[98] Bomb shelters, basically big steel tanks sunk in the ground, were stocked with canned food and water, radios, generators, Geiger counters to detect radiation, and special suits designed to protect people when they emerged days or weeks after a nuclear attack.

Likewise, schools held nuclear attack drills, teaching students to march into corridors or basements for safety or, if there was no time, to "duck and cover" by crouching under their desks. Today people realize that

TRUMAN AND THE ATOMIC BOMB

The United States never came close to using the atomic bomb during the Korean War, but U.S. officials included this terrible weapon with other contingency plans that never became reality. In a November 30, 1950, news conference, at a time when the mood in Washington, D.C., was never more desperate because Chinese troops were turning back the "Home by Christmas Offensive," a harried President Harry Truman made some ill-advised remarks that made news around the world. In MacArthur's War, *author Stanley Weintraub describes the sequence of questions that produced startling answers that, for a short time, scared many people around the world:*

"Truman: We will take whatever steps are necessary to meet the military situation, just as we always have.

Jack Dougherty, *New York Daily News:* Will that include the atomic bomb?

Truman: That includes every weapon that we have.

Paul R. Leach, *Chicago Daily News:* Mr. President, you said 'every weapon that we have.' Does that mean that there is active consideration of the use of the atomic bomb?

Truman: There has always been active consideration of its use. I don't want to see it used. It is a terrible weapon, and it should not be used on innocent men, women and children who have nothing to do with this military aggression [from China]. That happens when it's used.

[Questions shifted to other topics until veteran reporter Merriman Smith of United Press went back to the topic to clarify what the president had said.]

Smith: Did we understand you clearly, that the use of the atomic bomb is under active consideration?

Truman: Always has been Smitty, it's one of our weapons.

Robert Dixon, International News Service: Does that mean, Mr. President, use against military objectives or civilians?

Truman: It is a matter that the military people will have to decide."

In his book, Weintraub explains that news stories appearing the next day, that reported the United States was considering using the atomic bomb, made many other nations nervous, including its United Nations allies fighting in Korea. Weintraub believes that Truman made a mistake by talking at all about the atomic bomb, which was always a possible option but never a realistic one.

such drills would have done little to protect youngsters from a nuclear attack, but the fear of war with the Soviets was so real that it led Americans to overreact to the situation. Historian Martin Walker notes that this Cold War preoccupation carried over into popular culture:

> Take Hollywood's classic movie of the Red Menace, *I Was a Communist for the FBI*. It was made in 1951 based on the true story of Matt Cvetic, who had infiltrated the Communist Party in Pittsburgh. It won an Oscar nomination for best documentary. *Look* magazine ran a cover story, "Could the Reds Seize Detroit?" The Bowman gum company, famous for its baseball cards, brought out a new set of cards to go with its chewing-gum in 1951. Called "Children's Crusade against Communism," its slogan was "Fight the Red Menace."[99]

COMMUNISM AND POLITICS

The new Red Scare became an overriding issue in politics. As early as 1946, B. Carroll Reece, a Tennessee congressman and chairman of the Republican National Committee, stated that the fall elections would be a choice between "Communism and Republicanism."[100] A strong stand against Communism became a litmus test for candidates, helping newcomers like future president Richard Nixon who was elected to Congress that year by attacking his opponent, Helen Gahagan Douglas, as a Communist sympathizer.

When the war began, Truman, who in 1948 narrowly won reelection by defeating Republican Thomas Dewey, enjoyed support from both Republicans and Democrats. But when U.S. troops were embarrassed by early defeats, Republicans blamed Truman for the nation's weak defense even though members of both parties had voted for his military-shrinking budgets. As the war progressed, his political foes also criticized him for how the war was being conducted. When the Chinese entered the war just before the November 3 congressional elections and began battles that resulted in thousands of deaths and injuries to U.S. soldiers, Republicans like Illinois senate candidate Everett Dirksen viciously attacked Truman: "All the piety of the Administration will not put any life into the bodies of the young men coming back in wooden boxes."[101]

By election day, U.S. casualties in the war had topped twenty-eight thousand, a figure that did not include those from the Chinese offensive, and voters who were angry about the conflict voted scores of Democratic congressmen out of office. Despite criticism of his handling of the war, Truman never wavered in his belief that although it was important to help South Korea, he had to make sure the fighting did not expand to other nations.

In his memoirs, Truman wrote: "There was no doubt in my mind that we should not allow the action in Korea to extend to a general war. All-out military action against China had to be avoided, if for no other reason than because it was a gigantic booby trap."[102] But Truman had an increasingly difficult time doing that because of one man: Douglas MacArthur.

MacArthur vs. Truman

Most generals throughout U.S. history have been content to take orders from the president, whom the Constitution empowers as commander in chief of the armed forces. But in his 1958 book *Arms and the State*, Walter Mills explains that MacArthur was one of a few soldiers who tried to influence political policy:

> He was a military politician. From an early date he had taken a close interest in partisan politics; he was prepared to use his prestige as a soldier to influence civil policy decisions, and the arguments of military necessity to override the diplomatic or political objectives of his civilian superior.[103]

By the time the war started, the seventy-year-old MacArthur, a towering hero in World War II and the undisputed ruler of occupied Japan since then, had become accustomed to doing whatever he wanted, even if it meant ignoring orders from his superiors. This fatal flaw in a soldier led to a rift between MacArthur and Truman over how to conduct the war.

U.S. troops remove wounded from the Chosin Reservoir. As casualties continued to increase, President Truman received the blame for U.S. losses.

Although Truman wanted to keep Korea a "limited war," MacArthur as early as July 1950 publicly stated he would conquer the invaders and unify Korea, a mission that exceeded both U.S. and United Nations objectives. "I intend to destroy and drive back the North Korean forces," he said. "I may need to occupy all of North Korea."[104]

Although his brilliant plan to land at Inchon turned the tide of war in favor of UN forces, Gen. J. Lawton Collins, a member of the U.S. Army chief of staff at the time, claims its success further emboldened MacArthur to defy orders he disagreed with. Collins also believes it made other leaders hesitant to criticize him:

> The success of Inchon was so great, and the subsequent prestige of General MacArthur was so overpowering, that the Chiefs [of Staff] hesitated thereafter to question later plans and decisions of the general, which should have been challenged. In this we must share with General MacArthur some of the responsibility for actions that led to defeats in North Korea.[105]

THE WAR ANGERS AMERICANS

In America in the Korean War, *Edward F. Dolan provides a concise, vivid summation of the negative feelings the Korean War generated in Americans:*

"In the United States, the mounting criticism was new. Great segments of the public had originally seen Truman's defensive as a noble cause. But that nobility had been lost in the grim realities of war. Thousands of men . . . being torn from their homes and jobs as Reserve and National Guard Units were called for active duty. Other thousands were being drafted into the service. Daily, the country had to endure the press reports of soldiers dying or being maimed in battle. And, daily, the nation felt the economic pinch that accompanied any war. Taxes were increased to pay for its costs. Consumer goods made from materials needed for the war effort became scarce. Controls to freeze wages and prices to offset the danger of inflation were set. Worst of all, the failed offensive [in November 1950] had shattered the dream of a war quickly won. Millions were now asking: How long must our men go on fighting and losing their lives? Why are they fighting someone else's war? Why are they sacrificing themselves in a faraway backwater country?"

During the January to April 1951 counteroffensive, U.S. forces pushed the Chinese back across the 38th parallel.

Thus other U.S. military leaders remained silent when MacArthur split his forces prior to the "Home by Christmas" offensive, and when he disregarded directives to keep U.S. troops away from the Chinese border and not to bomb near the Yalu River. The latter two orders were both designed to prevent China from entering the war.

MacArthur also made careless, politically motivated statements that opposed Truman's policies and led to greater division over the war, such as the general's backing for a proposal by Chiang Kai-shek to allow Nationalist troops to fight in Korea, a move that would have inflamed Mao Tse-tung. In his memoirs, Truman wrote that he held back from firing MacArthur after the Chinese began beating UN forces because "I did not wish to have it appear as if he were being relieved because the offensive failed. I have never believed in going back on people when luck is against them."[106]

TRUMAN FIRES MACARTHUR

However, the Chinese triumphs at the end of 1950 which reclaimed all of North Korea and part of South Korea, including Seoul, were only temporary. After the initial shock at meeting the tough new foe and a series of humbling defeats, UN forces dug in and stopped the advancing enemy. From January to April 1951 a strengthened Eighth Army led by Gen. Matthew B. Ridgway mounted a powerful counteroffensive that once again hurled Communist forces north of the 38th parallel.

But the successes in March and April only further emboldened MacArthur, who renewed his backing for Nationalist troops, suggested using the atomic bomb against China, and in a series of interviews with the media criticized Truman's concept of a limited war, saying that only total victory was acceptable. Even worse, in late

March he undercut a planned attempt by Truman to begin talks to end the fighting. While the Truman administration was preparing a presidential announcement on possible negotiations, MacArthur, even though he had been advised of the effort, did something that sabotaged the planned peace initiative.

Without informing the JCS, MacArthur issued a statement to the news media on March 24 that derided China as a vastly overrated military power and predicted a UN victory. He also offered the Chinese an ultimatum to end the war before it proved even more costly for them:

> I stand ready at any time to confer in the field with the commander in chief of the enemy forces in an earnest effort to find any military means whereby the realization of the political objectives of the United Nations in Korea, to which no nation may justly take exception, might be accomplished without further bloodshed.[107]

The ill-timed statement undercut Truman's planned offer for peace talks, a move that might have shortened the war and saved thousands of lives; created confusion among allied countries as to who was directing American policy; and further divided the nation. MacArthur was now on shaky ground with Truman, who believed the general's overtures were a challenge to the power of the presidency, and he finally decided he had to get rid of MacArthur. But Truman did not act fast enough to stop the runaway general from exploding one final political bombshell.

On April 5, House minority leader Joseph Martin read a letter MacArthur sent him in which he agreed with Martin that Nationalist soldiers should fight in Korea. The general once again attacked Truman's concept of a limited war, claiming, "if we lose the war to Communism in Asia, the fall of Europe is inevitable. Win it and Europe most probably would avoid war and preserve freedom . . . there is no substitute for victory."[108]

Truman had taken his final insult from MacArthur. On April 11 the president announced that he had relieved MacArthur of his duties "so that there would be no doubt or confusion as to the real purpose and aim of our [war] policy."[109] It was a decision Truman had to make, but one for which he would pay a bitter penalty.

MacArthur Comes Home

MacArthur, who had been in the Pacific since before World War II, was treated to one of the most triumphant homecomings in U.S. history. Despite being sacked for what amounted to insubordination, the controversial general was still beloved by Americans, mainly because they remembered his leadership in World War II. A crowd of one hundred thousand cheered him when he landed in Honolulu, Hawaii, a half-million greeted him in San Francisco, California, and a Gallup Poll showed that Americans supported MacArthur over Truman 69 percent to 29 percent.

Angry telegrams attacking his dismissal flooded the White House (of 44,000 telegrams that arrived in the first 48 hours after Truman acted, only 300 supported him). And the *Chicago Tribune* was only one of many newspapers that criticized him: "President Truman must be impeached and convicted. . . . [The nation] is led by a fool who is surrounded by knaves."[110]

The MacArthur frenzy reached its pinnacle on April 19 when he addressed Congress. In one of the most famous speeches in U.S. history, the general refused to admit that he had made any mistakes, lied that the Joint Chiefs of Staff supported his policies, and ended the oration with a maudlin summation of his military career:

> I still remember the refrain of one of the most popular barracks ballads [of his youth], which proclaimed most profoundly that—"Old soldiers never die; they just fade away." And like the old soldier of that ballad, I now close my military career and just fade away—an old soldier who tried to do his duty as God gave him the light to see that duty. Good-bye.[111]

HARRY TRUMAN RECALLS GEN. DOUGLAS MACARTHUR

On April 11, 1951, when President Harry Truman dismissed Gen. Douglas MacArthur, he addressed the nation to explain his decision. The following excerpts from his speech are from The Department of State Bulletin:

"On defending his concept of 'limited war,' which MacArthur opposed, Truman said, 'In the simplest terms, what we are doing in Korea is this: We are trying to prevent a third world war. . . . The question we have had to face is whether the Communist plan of conquest can be stopped without general war. Our Government and other countries associated with us in the United Nations believe that the best chance of stopping it without general war is to meet the attack in Korea and defeat it there. That is what we have been doing. It is a difficult and bitter task. But so far it has been successful. So far, we have prevented World War III.'

On avoiding confusion over U.S. policy, he said 'A number of events have made it evident that General MacArthur did not agree with that policy [of limited war]. I have therefore considered it essential to relieve General MacArthur so that there would be no doubt or confusion as to the real purpose and aim of our policy. It was with the deepest personal regret that I found myself compelled to take this action. General MacArthur is one of our greatest military commanders. But the cause of world peace is more important than any individual.'"

MacArthur's speech drew the largest radio and television audience in history and garnered a reverent reaction from congressmen like Republican Dewey Short of Missouri, who proclaimed mystically, "We heard god speak here today, god in the flesh, the voice of god!"[112] But Speaker of the House Sam Rayburn of Texas, a Democrat, criticized MacArthur for trying to outmaneuver Truman: "We must never give up [the fundamental constitutional principle] that the military is subject to and under control of the civilian administration."[113]

The general's dismissal further politicized the war, and Congress began seven weeks of hearings on Truman's action with the general serving as the key witness. MacArthur's testimony was televised, but the longer Americans listened to him complain that U.S. setbacks had always been due to someone else's mistakes, never his, the more he began to "fade away." In *Truman*, biographer David McCullough writes that MacArthur grew "more shrill and vindictive, less like a hero, and his popular appeal declined."[114]

Douglas MacArthur's farewell speech before Congress is one of the most famous speeches in U.S. history.

McCarthyism

While MacArthur was creating problems for Truman overseas, the president had to contend with another opponent at home—U.S. Senator Joseph McCarthy, who embodied the hysteria over Communism and the divisive politics that plagued the nation during the Korean War. The Wisconsin Republican had been a political unknown until he delivered a startling Lincoln Day speech on February 9, 1950, in Wheeling, West Virginia. McCarthy created a national uproar that night when he claimed: "I have here in my hands a list of 205 names known to the Secretary of State [George Marshall] as being members of the Communist Party and who, nevertheless, are still working and shaping the policy of the State Department."[115]

McCarthy was lying—the list he held aloft did not name Communists in government—but his allegations gained him national fame, and for the next four years he waged a hateful campaign to punish people he believed to be Communists. Although some Communists working in the federal government were uncloaked during this period, McCarthy never uncovered any of them. Instead the Republican made unfounded, spiteful claims against Truman, his Democratic administration, and scores of other people. McCarthy labeled Secretary of State Dean Acheson "the Red Dean," called State Department Far East expert Owen Lattimore the "top Russian espionage agent in the United States," and stated that Secretary of State George C. Marshall, a revered World War II general, was "an instrument of the Soviet conspir-

acy."[116] None of his charges were ever proven true.

McCarthy's claims were so outrageous—he even claimed that Truman had been tricked into helping the Communists—it is hard to believe the public believed them. But in *The Fifties*, author David Halberstam writes that McCarthy succeeded because his charges "crystallized and politicized the anxieties of a nation living in a dangerous new era."[117] McCarthy remained a powerful, feared figure until 1954, when he charged in a series of televised hearings that the army itself was harboring Communists. By then even his fellow senators had had enough of his unfair tactics. On December 2, 1954, the Senate voted 67–22 to censure him for his unethical actions, claiming they were "contrary to senatorial traditions and tend to bring the Senate into disrepute."[118]

An alcoholic, McCarthy died in May 1957 of cirrhosis of the liver, but his name lives on in the term *McCarthyism*. In 1953, Truman defined it this way:

> The meaning of the word is the corruption of truth, the abandonment of our historical devotion to fair play. It is the abandonment of "due process" of law. It is the use of the big lie and the unfounded accusation against any citizen in the name of Americanism and security. It is the rise to power of the demagogue who lives on untruth; it is the spread of fear and the destruction of right in every level of our society . . . this horrible cancer is eating at the vitals of America and it can destroy the great edifice of freedom.[119]

Senator Joseph McCarthy—A Demagogue Exposed

In 1954, Americans started to turn against Senator Joseph McCarthy as they realized that almost all of the charges he made were false and were hurting innocent people. In the spring of 1954 during a televised hearing, the Wisconsin Republican had an ugly confrontation with Joseph Welch, a special counsel defending the U.S. Army against charges by McCarthy that Communists had infiltrated the Army. After McCarthy made unfounded accusations against a young lawyer in Welch's firm, Welch attacked the senator in blunt language that exposed how cruel McCarthy's tactics really were. His testimony is from Arthur Herman's Joseph McCarthy: Reexamining the Life and Legacy of America's Most Hated Senator:

"Until this moment, Senator, I think I never really gauged your cruelty or your recklessness. Fred Fisher [the young attorney] is starting what looks to be a brilliant career with us. Little did I dream you could be so reckless and so cruel as to do an injury to that lad. I fear he shall always bear a scar needlessly inflicted by you. Let us not assassinate this lad further, Senator. You have done enough. Have you no sense of decency, sir, at long last? Have you left no sense of decency?"

Herman goes on to explain that the televised incident helped further turn public sentiment against McCarthy. He notes that after the hearing, Fred Woltmann, who had once helped McCarthy with his investigations, began a column for the Scripps-Howard news service with the sentence: "Senator Joseph R. McCarthy has become a major liability to the cause of anti-Communism." It was the beginning of the end of McCarthyism.

HATRED OF THE WAR

McCarthy's tactics were an extension of the panic that gripped Americans during the Korean War, and one of their greatest fears was that their sons or daughters fighting in Korea would be killed. When this happened, people often directed their anger against Truman, the man they held responsible for involving the United States in Korea.

One father sent Truman a nasty note along with the medal his son was given after being killed in combat: "As you have been directly responsible for the loss of our son's life in Korea, you might just as well keep this emblem on display in your trophy room, a memory of one of your historic deeds."[120] This father's misery was symbolic of the many painful emotions the Korean War generated in Americans while it was being waged.

6 Waging Peace to End a War

A meeting in the spring of 1951 between George Kennan, one of the architects of America's Cold War policy, and Jacob Malik, the Soviet Union's ambassador to the United Nations, would lead to the beginning of the end of the Korean War. Kennan was on leave of absence from the State Department to write a book on U.S.–Soviet relations. But at the request of the Truman administration, he met on May 31 with Malik to offer the possibility of peace talks to end the war and avoid a deadly showdown between the two Cold War superpowers.

Malik, whose absence at UN Security Council meetings in June 1950 had allowed the United States to involve the UN in the war, now played a key part in opening peace talks. After listening to Kennan's proposal and conferring with his superiors in Moscow, Malik responded positively on June 23 in his first appearance on a UN radio broadcast. "The Soviet people," Malik said, "believe that, as a first step, discussions should be started among the belligerents for a cease-fire and an armistice providing for mutual withdrawal from the 38th Parallel."[121]

U.S. officials were still operating under the mistaken belief that the Soviets had ordered the North Koreans to attack South Korea. Although this was not true, the Soviets did wield a great deal of influence over their Communist counterparts in Asia, and within a week North Korea and China agreed to Malik's suggestion.

The first talks were held on July 10, but the fighting would drag on for two more years as both sides struggled to solve the thorny issues that divided them. There would also be a change of leadership in both the United States and the Soviet Union before peace was finally achieved—the election of Dwight D. Eisenhower as president and the death of Soviet premier Joseph Stalin.

WAR STALEMATE

When Gen. Matthew Ridgway took command of the Eighth Army in late 1950 following Gen. Walton Walker's death in a jeep accident, Ridgway was dismayed to discover that the troops he had inherited were lacking in confidence and spirit and retreating in fear from the advancing Chinese. After meeting in Tokyo with Gen. Douglas MacArthur, Ridgway arrived in

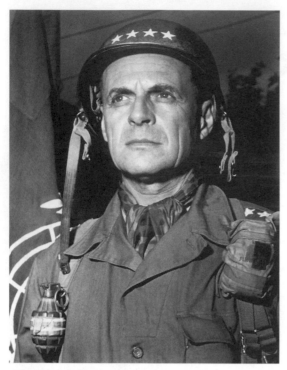

After MacArthur's dismissal, General Matthew B. Ridgway took command of the U.S. forces in Korea.

Korea on December 27 and immediately went to the front lines, telling everyone from privates to other generals what he expected of them. Years later, he described his stern message:

> I told them their soldier forebears would turn over in their graves if they heard some of the stories I had heard about the behavior of some of our troop leaders in combat. In time of battle, I wanted division commanders to be up with their forward battalions and I wanted corps commanders up with the regiment that was in the hottest action. If they had paperwork, they could do it at night. By day their place was up where the shooting was going on.[122]

His strong words and self-confident manner imparted a new fighting spirit to U.S. forces, but it would take them time to regroup. The Chinese greeted Ridgway on December 31 with a powerful new offensive, striking with tens of thousands of Communist soldiers across a forty-mile front north of Seoul. By January 5 they had captured Seoul again, and by January 15 they had pushed United Nations forces south to the 37th parallel.

But the UN's tough new commander was now ready to start fighting back. Ridgway ordered Operation Thunderbolt, an offensive in the west that began on January 25 and was the start of a turnaround that would last several months, include operations nicknamed "Killer" and "Ripper," and lead to Seoul's recapture on March 18, the final time the beleaguered South Korean capital would change hands.

When MacArthur was relieved of duty on April 11, Ridgway assumed command of UN forces, all U.S. troops in the Pacific, and occupied Japan. Ridgway, for one, was glad to see MacArthur go; he would no longer have to put up with brief battlefield visits by a general he believed came to Korea for "no purpose except to get photographs of [himself] with victorious troops."[123]

The two sides fought bitterly through the spring, attacking and counterattacking with deadly force, and by June 25 UN troops had established a defensive line that angled from forty miles north of the 38th parallel in the east to a few miles below it in the west. After just one year of war, both sides had already paid a terrible price—the UN command had four hundred thousand casualties while inflicting four times that number on the Communists—only to have Korea divided almost exactly as it had been before the fighting started. The two sides now faced each other across heavily fortified defensive positions that would vary only slightly until the end of the conflict, which for its final two years resembled the static "trench warfare" of World War I.

TRUCE TALKS

The first negotiating session took place on July 10 in Kaesong, a Communist-held town on the 38th parallel. The United States delegation was headed by Adm. C. Turner Joy and included ROK Maj. Gen. Paik Sun Yup, while the Communist contingent featured North Korean People's Army Lt. Gen. Nam Il and Chinese Gen. Hsieh Fang. Negotiators met in an ornate one-story teahouse, whose beautiful facade was marred by bullet holes and damage from artillery shells.

The two sides were wary and distrustful, quick to take offense at whatever was said, and overly concerned with symbolic gestures. Historian Stanley Sandler describes one absurdity of the opening session:

One year after the war began, the two sides still faced each other across heavily fortified defensive positions.

84984A

The Communists were [fanatical] regarding matters of precedent and "face." When the UN delegation brought in a small UN flag and stand to the meetings, the Communists responded with their own larger flag and stand. The erection of a modest UN sanitary facility led to a construction "war" with the Communists, who promptly built their own facility, brightly painted and landscaped as well.[124]

The talks continued until the Communists broke them off on August 23, claiming that UN forces had violated a noncombat zone that ringed Kaesong. When negotiations resumed two months later at nearby Panmunjom, about thirty miles northwest of Seoul, the two sides were still nearly as hostile as their soldiers, who were shooting at each other not many miles away.

A BRUTAL WAR

The peace talks would drag on for nearly two years, partly at the urging of Soviet leaders who knew that the war kept America from strengthening its forces in Europe. Premier Joseph Stalin admitted he was gleeful that "this war is getting on America's nerves," and in March 1952 the Soviet Politburo, the Communist Party's policy-making body, which Stalin controlled, passed a resolution stating, "We should not hurry the process of negotiations. It is not in our interest."[125]

But the talks were also slowed by the genuine animosity and hostility that negotiators brought to the peace sessions,

and the ill feeling that arose from an ugly, dirty war in which both sides acted with incredible brutality. In *Korea: The Unknown War*, Jon Halliday and Bruce Cumings claim:

> All sides in the war were guilty of atrocities. [North Korean] forces executed several hundreds of American prisoners of war, albeit usually in the traditional battlefield "humane" manner: one bullet behind the ear. The United Nations archives contain well-documented accounts, verified by witnesses and relatives, of several mass murders of southerners by the northern occupants. It has been alleged that the North Koreans perpetrated one of the greatest mass killings of the war in Taejon, where between 5,000 and 7,000 people were slaughtered and placed in mass graves.[126]

UN forces also committed acts of savagery against enemy soldiers and civilians that today seem indefensible. UN leaders, however, excused their actions by claiming that Korea was a guerrilla war, one in which enemy soldiers disguised themselves as civilians or used large refugee groups to cover their movements. It was a type of conflict twentieth-century U.S. soldiers had never experienced, a fact Marguerite Higgins of the *New York Herald-Tribune* pinpointed early in the fighting when she wrote, "This is no orthodox war."[127]

Americans described seeing advancing North Korean soldiers take off their uniforms and don the common white trousers and blouses worn by peasants. The impos-

THE BRIDGE AT NO GUN RI

In 1999, Associated Press writers Sang-hun Choe, Charles J. Hanley, and Martha Mendoza exposed the massacre of South Korean civilians by U.S. soldiers early in the Korean War. Their investigative series won a Pulitzer Prize, the most prestigious award in journalism, for uncovering the story nearly a half-century later through declassified documents and interviews with soldiers and civilians. Following is an excerpt from their articles from the Associated Press Internet site:

"It was a story no one wanted to hear: Early in the Korean War, villagers said, American soldiers machine-gunned hundreds of helpless civilians, under a railroad bridge in the South Korean countryside. When the families spoke out, seeking redress, they met only rejection and denial, from the U.S. military and their own government in Seoul. Now a dozen ex-GIs have spoken, too, and support their story with haunting memories from a 'forgotten' war. These American veterans of the Korean War say that in late July 1950, in the conflict's first desperate weeks, U.S. troops—young, green and scared—killed a large number of South Korean refugees, many of them women and children, trapped beneath a bridge at a place called No Gun Ri. In interviews with The Associated Press, ex-GIs speak of 100, 200 or simply hundreds dead. The Koreans, whose claim for compensation was rejected [in 1998], say 300 were shot to death at the bridge and 100 died in a preceding air attack. American soldiers, in their third day at the warfront, feared North Korean infiltrators [were] among the fleeing South Korean peasants, veterans said. 'It was assumed there were enemy in these people,' ex-rifleman Herman Patterson of Greer, S.C., told the AP. American commanders had ordered units retreating through South Korea to shoot civilians as a defense against disguised enemy soldiers, according to once-classified documents found by the AP in months of researching U.S. military archives and interviewing veterans across the United States. Six veterans of the 1st Cavalry Division said they fired on the refugee throng . . . 'We just annihilated them,' said ex-machine gunner Norman Tinkler of Glasco, Kan. [However] . . . some soldiers refused to shoot what one described as 'civilians just trying to hide.'"

sibility of being able to tell friend from foe, innocent villager from disguised enemy soldier, forced U.S. troops to make difficult decisions when they encountered Koreans who *appeared* to be refugees. In stories for *Time* and *Life* magazines, John Osborne commented that the Communist guerrilla tactics:

. . . force upon our men in the field acts and attitudes of the utmost savagery. This means not the usual, inevitable savagery of combat in the field but savagery in detail—the blotting out of villages where the enemy *may* be hiding; the shooting and shelling of refugees who *may* include North Koreans in the anonymous white clothing of the Korean countryside, or who *may* be screening an enemy march upon our positions.[128]

During the war the news media did not detail UN atrocities, but in 1999 reporters for the Associated Press combined declassified military documents and interviews with U.S. soldiers and South Korean civilians to explain an incident that occurred July 26–29, 1950, in the village of No Gun Ri. In an investigative series that won a Pulitzer Prize, AP writers described how three hundred men, women, and children were shot to death by U.S. soldiers who could not tell if they were refugees or the enemy.

Soldiers at No Gun Ri were among units of the First Cavalry Division who were acting under the following order: "No refugees to cross the front lines. Fire everyone trying to cross lines. Use discretion in case of women and children."[129] In effect, soldiers had a license to kill civilians, and they did. (No Gun Ri is believed to be the second worst incident in U.S. military history, ranking only behind Vietnam's My Lai massacre in 1968 in which soldiers killed up to five hundred noncombatants.)

GOOKS

These acts of brutality are hard to comprehend today. But experts agree that during any war, soldiers become calloused to death and destruction by being exposed to it every day. They also build up a tremendous rage against enemies who have shot or maimed their friends and are still trying to kill them, anger that often overrides their better judgment when dealing with the opposing side.

Reginald Thompson, a British war correspondent, however, believes that another factor led Americans to do things they would later regret. He notes that U.S. soldiers called all Koreans "gooks," a racist term referring to Asians in general that was also used during World War II. Thompson said the word's racist connotations dehumanized civilians they encountered: "Americans called Koreans gooks [because] otherwise these essentially kind and generous Americans would not have been able to kill them indiscriminately or smash up their homes and poor belongings."[130]

Korean War historian John Toland believes the degrading term was part of a widespread, generally racist attitude U.S. soldiers held toward Koreans. He says,

> Most young American soldiers arriving in Korea were led to believe that the Koreans were an inferior, ignorant, thieving bunch of people—"gooks." Few knew anything at all about Korean history or culture, and almost all were totally perplexed when a Korean would say, "Me no gook. *You* gook." In Korean the word *Miguk* meant "American."[131]

But the Chinese also stereotyped and demeaned U.S. soldiers on a racial basis. In a pamphlet printed for its troops, the Chinese claimed that American soldiers:

> Are weak, afraid to die, and haven't the courage to attack or defend. They depend on their planes, tanks and artillery. . . . They will cringe when, if on the advance, they hear firing. . . . If defeated, they have no orderly formation. Without the use of their mortars they become completely lost . . . they become dazed and completely demoralized.[132]

THE POW ISSUE

The brutal behavior in combat and the racist attitudes both sides held toward each other extended to prisoners of war (POWs), who are supposed to be treated humanely after being captured. Sandler writes that the North Koreans and Chinese subjected Americans to inhumane conditions, including torture:

> U.S. POWs, usually survivors of a number of "death marches" [between prison camps] were paraded through

U.S. troops referred to all Koreans as "gooks," a term that helped them justify the brutal killing not only of soldiers but of civilians as well.

the streets of Pyongyang. Their haggard, emaciated forms were frequently photographed and those photographs were given global distribution. Thus the North Koreans documented their own barbarism. Those who survived the death marches and the shooting found themselves in camps in the far North with a continued ordeal of beatings, near-starvation and unrelenting physical and mental pressure to turn "progressive" and broadcast or write messages back home denouncing American "aggression" in Korea.[133]

The treatment of North Korean POW by their UN captors was not much better. At the end of 1951, General Ridgway reported that an estimated six thousand POWs had died in UN camps, mainly from starvation. Historians Jon Halliday and Bruce Cumings explain that after the United States proposed in negotiating sessions in 1951 that POWs should have the right to choose not to return home after the war, conditions in UN camps became much worse:

> From this point on there were major revolts among prisoners against pressure on them not to return home. For a period there was, in theory, a process termed "screening" that . . . would allow a prisoner to opt for or against repatriation. In fact . . . "screening" often meant intimidation and torture. Many POWs were forcibly tattooed with anti-Communist slogans to make it more difficult for them to choose to return home. . . . The USA's first chief negotiator at the peace talks, Admiral

Joy, [wrote that] anyone who expressed a wish to return home was "either beaten black and blue or killed . . . the majority of the POWs were too terrified to frankly express their choice."[134]

THE TALKS GO ON

When talks resumed in October 1951, two main issues divided negotiators: (1) the Chinese sought restoration of the 38th parallel as the border between the two Koreas while U.S. officials wanted the existing battle line, which in places was north of that; and (2) how to handle the release of POWs. UN forces held 171,000 prisoners, 50,000 of whom claimed they did not want to go home, while the Communists had far fewer. Negotiations on those issues were frustrating for U.S. officials, who wanted to end the war but kept running into Chinese obstinance. In January 1952, Truman commented on the stalled talks in his diary, writing, "Dealing with Communist governments is like an honest man trying to deal with a numbers racket king or the head of a dope ring."[135]

The POW issue became the major stumbling block in reaching an agreement. The Communists wanted all their POWs returned when fighting ended, but U.S. officials sought "voluntary" repatriation because so many of them did want to stay in the south. The Communists would not accept this, believing it would be a tremendous blow to their pride if some of their soldiers refused to come home, but Truman

BRAINWASHING

When the Korean War ended, one of the most horrifying aspects that emerged about life in prisoner of war camps was how Communist captors tried to break down their prisoners, mentally and physically, in a technique given the name brainwashing. This type of torture was used in attempts to convert prisoners to Communism, make them issue statements criticizing their country's involvement in the war, or confess to alleged war crimes. In The Wars of America *by Robert Leckie, Dr. Charles Mayor, a U.S. delegate to the United Nations, details the inhumane conditions used in this form of torture:*

"It is a method obviously calculated by the Communists to bring a man to the point where a dry crust of bread or a few hours' uninterrupted sleep is a great event in his life. . . . The total picture presented is one of human beings reduced to a status lower than that of animals, filthy, full of lice, festered wounds full of maggots, their sickness regulated to a point just short of death, unshaven, without haircuts or baths for as much as a year, men in rags, exposed to the elements, fed with carefully measured minimum quantities and the lowest quality of food and unsanitary water served often in rusty cans, isolated, faced with squads of trained interrogators, deprived of sleep and browbeaten with mental anguish."

POWs after their release. While held captive, POWs suffered all types of abuse.

argued, "We will not buy an armistice by turning over human beings for slaughter and slavery."[136] The failure to compromise on the issue meant that the Korean War dragged on for an additional eighteen months, resulting in another 32,000 U.S. casualties, including 9,000 deaths.

New U.S. and Soviet Leaders

While the talks and the war dragged on in Korea, the big event in America in 1952 was the November presidential election, with the war being the campaign's major issue. Because Truman decided not to run, the

Americans viewed Dwight D. Eisenhower as a heroic figure who would bring the U.S. forces home from Korea.

pledge he made on October 24 in Detroit, Michigan, during a radio and television campaign speech broadcast to the entire nation. He criticized the Korean War as "the burial ground of twenty-one-thousand American dead,"[137] and vowed to

> ... bring the Korean War to an early and honorable end. That is my pledge to the American people. . . . That job requires a personal trip to Korea. I shall make that trip. Only in that way could I learn how best to serve the American people in the cause of peace. I shall go to Korea.[138]

The Republican was triumphant, winning almost seven million more votes than Stevenson. In early December the president-elect fulfilled his dramatic promise with a three-day visit to Korea during which he reviewed troops, trod ice-covered battlefields, visited the wounded in Mobile Army Surgical Hospital (MASH) units, and was reunited with his son, John, a major.

Eisenhower became the nation's thirty-fourth president on January 20, 1953. He had promised to end the war quickly, but the fighting would continue for another six months. There were no major attacks or counterattacks, just a steady series of small, deadly, military actions that took lives while only slightly rearranging the defensive line established in the summer of 1951.

race pitted Democratic Illinois governor Adlai Stevenson against Eisenhower. Americans perceived the former World War II general who had guided Allied forces to victory in Europe as a strong, heroic figure, one who could ease them out of a war that many no longer wanted to fight. Voters were also more comfortable with the homespun Eisenhower—the twentieth century's most famous campaign slogan, "I Like Ike," summed up his warm appeal—than the intellectual Stevenson. They also wanted a change after twenty years of Democratic leadership.

Many historians believe one of the reasons Eisenhower won was a startling

STALIN DIES

Another leadership change in the Soviet Union two months later, however, would prove to be even more significant to ending the war than the election of Eisenhower. A key event in jump-starting the stalled talks came on March 5, 1953, when Stalin died of a stroke after nearly three decades in power. Ten days later his successor, Georgi M. Malenkov, gave new hope for peace in Korea when he said his country believed it could settle disputes with any nation, including its archenemy the United States, through peaceful negotiations. Although the Soviet Union was not officially a participant in the war, it exerted a tremendous amount of control over other Communist nations. Malenkov's more conciliatory attitude influenced China and North Korea, which soon became more willing to compromise on war issues.

On March 26, after many refusals, Chinese and North Korean officials finally consented to a request from U.S. Gen. Mark Clark—who replaced Gen. Matthew Ridgway as commander of UN forces in Korea in 1951—to exchange sick and wounded prisoners. Four days later, Chinese leader Chou En-lai made an even more astonishing offer, one that would lead to resolution of the POW controversy:

THE DEMILITARIZED ZONE

In The Korean War: History and Tactics, *David Rees explains that the defensive lines between the two sides were static for the final two years of the Korean War. This is his description of how Communist and UN forces dug in and fortified their defensive lines:*

"Stretching 155 miles across the peninsula of Korea the military lines of the two sides were fashioned for a static war that reflected their different strengths and weaknesses. . . . The Communists were forced to use the reverse slopes of the hills they held by their inferiority in firepower. Into these reverse slopes, safe from the hands of the expertly handled UN artillery, they dug [systems of] tunnels and caves to house an army of 850,000 men . . . their posts built in a fortified belt 15 to 25 miles deep. In contrast to the Communist effort, the UN [line] was much less substantial. Because of the weight of UN firepower it took the form of a simple trench and bunker line slashed into the forward slopes of the North-held hill crests. To provide some sort of cushion in front of the [line] itself, there were a number of fortified outposts at some distance forward of the line. . . . The disadvantage of the UN position was that they were so shallow. At any time a determined and sudden Chinese attack could push UN troops off [back]. . . . This situation gave rise to the numerous bloody little battles for position which formed the only major actions of the stalemated war."

How Many Americans Died in the Korean War?

When the Korean War ended, the United States reported that 54,246 soldiers died in combat. Yet in 2000, it was discovered that the real death toll was 36,940 because a government worker nearly a half-century earlier had incorrectly added up the fatalities. In a story in Time *magazine, Mark Thompson explains what happened:*

"It seems that the higher figure—engraved on the five-year-old KOREAN WAR VETERANS MEMORIAL on the National Mall in Washington—cropped up shortly after both sides declared a truce in 1953 and has been repeated, erroneously, ever since. The 'primary culprit' was an anonymous government clerk, the Pentagon says. The bureaucrat mistakenly added all nonbattlefield U.S. military deaths—20,617—that occurred worldwide during the three-year conflict to the more than 33,000 U.S. battlefield dead in Korea. But only 3,275 of those nonbattlefield deaths—largely due to accidents or disease—occurred in Korea. In a rare example of interservice cooperation, a Pentagon memo notes, 'All service historian offices have been advised . . . and are in agreement with the revision.'"

A lone bugler plays taps at a military cemetery, honoring the Americans killed in Korea.

Both parties to the negotiations should undertake to repatriate, immediately after the cessation of hostilities, all those prisoners of war in their custody who insist upon repatriation, and to hand over the remaining POWs to a neutral state so as to ensure a just solution to the question of their repatriation.[139]

Peace at Last

The Chinese decision to accept a repatriation compromise was the beginning of the end of the Korean War. The two sides resumed negotiations at Panmunjom on April 26, and three days later, in fulfillment of the deal struck with General Clark, 149

Americans, 64 other UN soldiers, and 471 ROK POWs were released in exchange for ten times that many Communists. That prisoner trade made the two delegations even more anxious to end the war, and on June 8 they finally worked out an agreement on repatriation and declared a truce. The cease-fire to end fighting was scheduled for July 27, 1953, three years and thirty-two days after the conflict began.

The POW agreement permitted prisoners to return home within sixty days, with no force or threats allowed to convince them not to return. Operation Big Switch began on August 5 at Panmunjom, and within a month the United Nations had handed over 75,823 prisoners (5,640 of them Chinese) while the Communists returned 12,773 (3,597 Americans and 7,862 South Koreans, the rest from other nations).

Those not choosing repatriation were turned over to the Neutral Nations Repatriation Committee, which allowed them ninety days more to consider their decision. In the end, 21,809 Communist POWs—14,227 Chinese and 7,582 Koreans—chose to stay in South Korea or go to Nationalist-controlled Formosa. Of the UN prisoners, slightly more than 300 decided not to return home—21 Americans, 325 Koreans, and 1 British soldier.

The Communists were embarrassed that so many of their soldiers refused to return home, but the truce terms proved even less satisfying for the United States: North Korea would remain a Communist threat to South Korea, and there would be no real peace agreement, simply a cessation of hostilities. The military line the two sides held at war's end, which cut across Korea from north of the 38th parallel in the east to south of it in the west, became the new border between the two countries and gave South Korea a net gain of about 1,500 square miles. A demilitarized (no-fire) zone 1.2 miles wide was also created along the new boundary to keep the two sides apart.

The war had been fought to a stalemate, becoming the first armed conflict the United States had failed to win. Truman, for one, groused that if he had agreed to the same peace terms while president, "they [Republicans] would have tried to draw and quarter me."[140] He was probably right, but Eisenhower's status as a war hero gave him the political strength to consent to a draw with a Communist opponent that many believed America should have easily defeated. Also, Americans by then were so sick of the war they were willing to accept any conditions to end the fighting.

A PLEASANT SILENCE

The day the truce was signed, Anthony Ebron, a corporal in the First Marine Division, was on the front lines. He says the sound of silence on the battlefield convinced him the war was over.

> Those last few days were pretty bloody. Each time we thought the war was over we'd go out and fight again. The day it ended? We shot off so much artillery that day the ground shook. One of my best buddies was killed that day by a Commie artillery round. Then, that night, the noise just stopped. We knew it was over.[141]

Chapter

7 Aftermath: The War with No Peace

Although the fighting stopped in 1953, the Korean War did not end for eighty-seven-year-old Hong Chil-soon until August 15, 2000, when she once again held the daughter she had given up for dead a half century earlier. Hugging Kim Ok Bae, who had been spirited away by invading North Korean soldiers, Hong said through a tearful embrace, "Thank you so much for being alive! Thank the dear leader for taking care of you!"[142]

This touching scene was one of many after a plane from the North landed peacefully in Seoul for the first time since before the Korean War, reuniting one hundred passengers with family members they had not seen for five decades. The term "dear leader" was a surprisingly warm reference to Kim Jong Il, who became North Korea's premier in 1994 upon the death of his father Kim Il Sung. The same plane flew north later that day to bring together another one hundred mothers, fathers, brothers, and sisters who were among the estimated ten million Koreans separated by the war.

The reunions were part of a series of amazing breakthroughs North and South Korea made in 2000 toward normalizing relations and, perhaps, eventual reunification. The truce declared on July 27, 1953, had ended the fighting, but not the ideo-

logical battle that continued to divide the two halves of Korea. A *New York Times* story on the cease-fire signing at Panmunjom predicted the problems that the two Koreas and the rest of the world would continue to face:

> The ceremony, attended by representatives of sixteen members of the United Nations, took precisely eleven minutes. Then the respective delegations walked from the meeting place without a word or handshake between them. The matter-of-fact procedure underlined what spokesmen of both sides emphasized: That though the shooting would cease within twelve hours after the signing, only an uneasy armed truce and political difficulties, perhaps even greater than those of the armistice negotiations, were ahead.[143]

The continuing division of Korea, however, was the least significant of the many changes the war became a catalyst for throughout the world. The bitter legacy of this bitter battle would force the United States into an even more divisive conflict in Vietnam; profoundly alter the futures of China, Japan, and other Asian nations; intensify the Cold War in Europe and Asia;

and ignite a frightening arms race between the United States and the Soviet Union.

AMERICA'S NEW ROLE

A decade after it had hesitated to enter World War II to save Europe from Germany because of its belief in isolationism (the theory that America was better off not becoming involved in the problems of other countries), the United States in 1950 sent soldiers to fight and die in a little-known Asian nation. In *Korea: The Untold Story of the War*, Joseph C. Goulden claims that this act pushed the United States into a more active role in international affairs, one it has never been able to relinquish:

It was the turning point for America's post–World War II military and diplomatic strategy. Korea marked the first time the United States went to arms to attempt to halt Communist military expansion. Korea was the first step on a long road of such ventures; indeed,

After being separated for fifty years, a North Korean man is reunited with his South Korean mother on August 15, 2000.

two months after the start of fighting there, the United States would send its first military aid to the French, who were fighting an insurgency [by Communists] in Indochina that ultimately was to become the Vietnam War. In the next decades, for better or worse, America was to commit increasing amounts of its national resources—and prestige—to Southeast Asia, to Europe, to Africa, to Latin America. The Korean War marked the start of the construction of a military juggernaut, the support of which consumed half the annual federal budget, even in "peacetime" years, and found American men and women at posts in the farthest reaches of the world.[144]

For the remainder of the twentieth century, a nation once content to sit idly on the sidelines while other nations warred against one another or suffered catastrophes such as earthquakes and droughts would send money, soldiers, or both to combat those problems. America would usually act in concert with the United Nations, a partnership President Harry S. Truman forged in 1950 when he deliberately involved it in the Korean War.

THE VIETNAM WAR

This new American attitude became apparent shortly after the Korean War ended. When nineteen nations met in Geneva, Switzerland, in 1954 to consider the lingering problems in Korea as well as Indochina—the former French colonies that today comprise Vietnam, Cambodia, and Laos—President Dwight D. Eisenhower and other U.S. officials began to lead the nation into an eerily similar, equally unwinnable war in Vietnam.

In May of that year, the Communists in Vietnam led by Ho Chi Minh had defeated French forces in a fierce battle at Dien Bien Phu to end decades of colonial rule. In Geneva the United States and other western nations, desperate once again to stop Communists from taking over an entire country, decided to divide Vietnam in the same way that Korea and Germany had been divided after World War II. Even though this process had already proven disastrous in both of those nations, the former French colony was partitioned into North and South Vietnam, and reunification elections were planned for 1956. But as in Korea the elections were never held, which meant creation, once again, of two opposed nations—one Communist and one non-Communist—set on an irreversible course toward war.

In *Korea: The Unknown War*, authors Jon Halliday and Bruce Cumings comment, "Korea had a profound effect on U.S. strategic thinking and led straight into Vietnam."[145] American involvement in Vietnam, which started with more than $1 billion in military aid to France during its battle with the Communists, progressed from helping South Vietnam remain a democracy to a full-scale war that took the lives of 58,000 Americans and divided the nation more severely than at any time since the Civil War.

THE DOMINO THEORY

The Korean War was only a prelude to the even more controversial and divisive Vietnam War. A major factor that led to U.S. involvement in Vietnam, a second guerrilla war in East Asia that the United States was fated not to win, was the "domino theory." President Dwight D. Eisenhower defined the term in 1954 when it appeared Communist forces were going to defeat the French in Vietnam. In The Fifties, *David Halberstam discusses the rationale behind this theory, which claimed that if Vietnam turned Communist, other Southeast Asian nations would soon follow:*

"At one point in early April, [Eisenhower] wrote [Winston] Churchill a surprisingly passionate letter asking him to join in united action [to help the French]: 'If I may refer again to history; we failed to halt [Japanese Emperor] Hirohito, [Italy's Benito] Mussolini and [Germany's Adolf] Hitler by not acting in unity and in time. That marked the beginning of many years of stark tragedy and desperate peril. May it not be that our nations have learned something from that lesson?' A few days later at a press conference, he outlined for the first time what became known as the domino theory: 'You have a row of dominoes set up, you knock over the first one, and what will happen to the last one is the certainty that it will go over very quickly. So you could have the beginning of a disintegration [nation after nation falling to Communism] that would have the most profound consequences.'"

THE ARMS RACE

America's new global mission in opposing Communism in places like Korea and Vietnam forced the government to drastically boost defense spending so the military could perform its new duties around the world. At first the huge expenditures fueled the U.S. economy, helping America continue its dramatic post–World War II economic boom. Rearmament during the Korean War, for example, led to a huge expansion of the U.S. economy; the nation's annual gross national product (GNP), its overall economic output, increased $60 billion between 1950 and 1953, twice the amount that defense spending rose.

But the massive expense of Korea, Vietnam, and other new global missions led to higher taxes and decades of deficit spending by the government (spending more than it collected in taxes), which by the 1970s began to weaken the U.S. economy. Even George F. Kennan, who first laid the philosophical foundation for America's containment policy, would later realize that the Cold War price tag had been too high. In a 1995 essay, Kennan noted:

We paid with 40 years of enormous and otherwise unnecessary military expenditures. We paid through the cultivation of nuclear weaponry to the point where the vast and useless nuclear arsenals had become (and remain today) a danger to the very environment of the planet.[146]

The most expensive and frightening part of the defense buildup was a nuclear arms race with the Soviet Union, which in 1951 trailed the United States in atomic bombs 450 to 24. The United States escalated this deadly contest on November 1, 1952, when it exploded the first hydrogen bomb, a nuclear device many times more powerful than the original atomic bomb, and for the next four decades the Cold War opponents vied to see which could stockpile the most nuclear weapons.

By the time this costly competition ended in the late 1980s, the two nations had amassed enough nuclear bombs and missiles to destroy the world several times over, even though both knew it would be suicide to start such a war. Even worse, by the end of the twentieth century several other nations including China and North Korea had joined the nuclear weapons fraternity, raising new fears about a possible nuclear holocaust that could destroy mankind.

INTEGRATING THE MILITARY

One of the few positive results of the Korean War was that it forced the armed forces to finally implement President Truman's 1948 order to integrate the military.

Although the various branches of the military had made a sluggish start, most units in 1950 were still segregated, which meant that African-American soldiers were still not receiving equal treatment with whites, a condition they also faced in civilian life during this period of U.S. history.

One reason Korea speeded up integration was that the Twenty-fourth Infantry Regiment, famous for "bugging out" early in the war, was an all-black unit commanded by white officers. African-American units like this one were more poorly trained, supplied, and led than all-white units, factors that combined to negatively affect their battle performance. U.S. military officials who had been hesitant about integration began to realize that they needed to mix black and white soldiers together to make the units stronger.

General J. Lawton Collins, for one, argued that, "Negro soldiers, when properly trained and fully integrated with their white comrades, would fight as well and would readily be accepted as equals."[147] When units were integrated, Collins' prediction about improved performance by African-American soldiers came true. A second factor that forced greater integration was that the Army needed African-American soldiers to rebuild white military units depleted by combat.

CHINA AND JAPAN

Although America did not get many other benefits from the Korean War, Asia's two

ARMY INTEGRATION

In 1950, African Americans encountered as much segregation in the military as they did in civilian life. During the Korean War, however, the armed forces finally implemented Harry Truman's 1948 presidential order to integrate the services. In The Forgotten War: America in Korea, 1950–1953, *military historian Clay Blair explains the segregation African-American soldiers had to endure before the Korean War forced the services to utilize all of its soldiers and combine segregated units with all-white units:*

"The history of blacks in the Army was a long and shameful tale, more or less paralleling black history in American civil life. The Army had never wanted black soldiers. But in the Civil War, World War I, and World War II, political and other circumstances compelled it to accept large numbers of blacks. . . . When the Korean War broke out the Army was still rigidly segregated and racist. Owing to the drastic shrinkage in its size and the majority view that large black units were undesirable, Congress had relieved the Army of its obligation to maintain four black regiments. Of the four 'traditional' black regiments, only the 24th Infantry [an important part of the 25th Division] in Japan remained, and it survived mainly because its large structure was required to absorb the many blacks in Japan and because [most officers] wanted the blacks out of sight and in one place. The 24th Infantry was thus a legacy of the shameful treatment of blacks in the U.S. Army."

An all-black unit moves up to the firing line in Korea. The U.S. Army was still segregated when the war broke out.

most powerful nations, China and Japan, both gained immeasurably from the conflict. China, only a year after its creation as a Communist nation, won new world stature for battling the United States to a draw. In Japan, U.S. and UN spending on the conflict greatly strengthened that country's war-ravaged economy. In *The Korean War: History and Tactics*, consulting editor David Rees writes:

> China's intervention in Korea and its initial victories over [Douglas] Mac-Arthur's forces made the new China a world power. . . . By its resistance in Korea, China was to become a formidable counterweight to Moscow within the world Communist movement. China now sought its own voice in world affairs; the death of [Joseph] Stalin in the closing months of the Korean War made Mao Tse-tung the political equal of any subsequent Soviet leader.[148]

China also used the proximity of U.S. troops to its border in October 1950 as an excuse to seize neighboring Tibet, but the war also had negative consequences for this new Asian power. In *Korea: The Unknown War*, Jon Halliday and Bruce Cumings write, "For China it caused many deaths and much suffering and kept China out of the United Nations for two decades."[149] Mao's favorite son, Mao An-ying, was one of the dead, killed in a bombing raid on Pyongyang in November 1950.

The wartime benefits were almost as great for Japan, an enemy of the United States only a few years earlier. "The Korean war," according to Cold War historian Mar-

tin Walker, "transformed the role, the status, and the economy of Japan."[150] In three years, U.S. and UN purchases in Japan for everything from ships and trucks to medicine totaled $3.5 billion, which more than doubled its manufacturing output.

The massive cash infusion continued America's post–World War II goal of changing Japan from a bitter enemy to a staunch ally against Communism. As early as January 6, 1948, U.S. Army secretary Kenneth Royall stated, "We are building in Japan a self-sufficient democracy, strong enough and stable enough to support itself and at the same time serve as a deterrent against any other totalitarian war threat which might hereafter arise in the Far East."[151] The Korean War simply speeded up that process.

A Shattered Korea

Although both halves of Korea claimed victory when the cease-fire took effect, survivors on both sides were surrounded by death and destruction. Both nations suffered tremendous devastation, South Korea from ground battles the first year and North Korea from combat and relentless aerial bombing that intensified the longer the war continued. As early as 1951, when he testified before Congress after being dismissed by President Harry S. Truman, Gen. Douglas MacArthur admitted that the damage already done in South Korea sickened him:

> The war in Korea has almost destroyed that nation. I have never seen such devastation. I have seen, I guess, as much blood and disaster as any living man,

DEATH AND DESTRUCTION

The Korean War created more death and destruction in one small country than any conflict ever had. In Korea: The Unknown War, *authors Jon Halliday and Bruce Cumings explain the devastation from three years of fighting:*

"The people of Korea suffered worst in this war, especially civilians in the North, who had to live three years under the heaviest and most sustained bombing ever known, and the millions of refugees who wandered desperately across the blasted landscape of their beautiful country. . . . The total number of people killed was almost certainly well over 3 million—possibly more like 4 million—in a nation whose population was some 30 million when the war started. Although these figures may seem high, if one takes into account the almost unbelievable intensity of the bombing, the shortage of medical facilities, the lack of food and the extreme cold and lack of shelter in the context of a scorched-earth policy and the systematic destruction of livestock, they are not implausible. By far the largest number died in North Korea. . . . Our estimate is that over 2 million North Korean civilians died and about 500,000 North Korean soldiers. In addition, some 1 million Chinese soldiers probably died (although one firsthand Chinese source has put the figure at 3 million). South Korean civilian deaths were about 1 million; Southern battle-related deaths were some 47,000; nonbattle-related military deaths were probably higher."

and it just curdled my stomach the last time I was there. After I looked at that wreckage and those thousands of women and children and everything, I vomited.[152]

Historians estimate that the war took the lives of as many as four million North and South Koreans, a huge number considering that only 30 million people lived in the two countries before the fighting started. And the bloodshed had not solved anything.

U.S. officials signed the armistice with the Communists, but South Korean president Syngman Rhee refused, claiming that he would observe it for only ninety days and then might start fighting again. Rhee opposed the cease-fire because he wanted to continue the war until North Korea was destroyed. To gain his cooperation, the United States, which had installed him in power after World War II, signed a mutual defense pact with South Korea in August 1953. In effect, America took control of the

South Korean army and committed itself to maintaining troops there to defend that nation. In 2000, a force of thirty-seven thousand U.S. soldiers was still stationed there.

Rhee remained in power until 1960, when he was ousted by South Koreans who were angry about his increasingly oppressive regime (he died in exile in Hawaii four years later), but the country remained democratic under a succession of leaders. In North Korea, Kim Il Sung ruled until his death. But the paths the two countries took to the year 2000 were vastly different.

NORTH AND SOUTH KOREA

From the end of the war to the end of the twentieth century, South Korea evolved into a stable democracy with one of East Asia's most vibrant economies. This remarkable turnaround was due to the hard work of its people and massive infusions of

North Korean students walk past a statue of Kim Il Sung (top) as prosperous South Koreans shop in a Seoul department store (right). Although life in the North remains harsh, South Korea has grown to become the world's twelfth largest economy.

U.S. aid. In *Outposts of Empire: Korea, Vietnam, and the Origins of the Cold War in Asia, 1949–1954*, Steven Hugh Lee writes that American officials decided to make South Korea strong and prosperous:

> The enthusiasm accompanying the U.S. efforts to rehabilitate Korea were truly amazing and fueled [America's] world struggle against Communism. The post-armistice era in Korea was seen as a showcase of America's power and wealth. In a meeting with fourteen other nations that had participated in the conflict, [Secretary of State John Foster] Dulles revealed that the United States was "extremely anxious to start the economic rehabilitation of South Korea in a way that would be impressive not only in Asia but throughout the world as an example of what the free nations can do."[153]

South Korea by 2000 had the world's twelfth largest economy, with a per capita income of $13,200 annually, about twelve times the North's estimated $1,090. Its nearly 47 million citizens enjoyed a standard of living comparable to people living in western nations, complete with such modern-day amenities as cellphones, CD players, and computers, all manufactured by South Korean firms such as Samsung. Lee Ae Ran, a thirty-six-year-old North Korean defector, was amazed at how much more comfortable life was in South Korea. "Everything here is filled with wonder,"[154] Lee said in 2000, three years after she fled her Communist homeland, where most people did not even have telephones in their homes.

Life in North Korea after the war was much harsher and bleaker under Kim Il Sung, who not only wielded complete control but forced his people to revere him almost as a god, as did Chairman Mao in China. After Kim died on July 8, 1994, David E. Sanger wrote in a *New York Times* story:

> For half a century, North Korea has been essentially a family business headed by Kim, whose image is captured in monuments in every town and who is credited, in the national mythology and in song, with the country's creation and development. His cult of personality is everywhere, celebrated in "mass games" run on his birthday that involve hundreds of thousands, and in the everyday invocation of his philosophy of "juche" or national self-reliance.[155]

North Korea's economy was strong until the Cold War waned at the end of the twentieth century, when the Soviet Union broke apart and China began to adopt more liberal economic policies. After those nations cut off aid to North Korea, its economy began crumbling and by 1999 its 21 million inhabitants were struggling to survive from day to day. In addition to energy shortages, power failures, and a lack of funds to purchase international products it could not produce, North Korea had such severe food shortages that some experts believe as many as 2.5 million people died of famine there during the late 1990s.

This disparity in lifestyles was similar to that which existed between East and West Germany—two other nations split apart after World War II—before they overcame four decades of division to reunite in 1990. But it would not be until the fiftieth anniversary of the Korean War that the two

Koreas would dare consider a similar historic step.

CAN KOREA BE REUNIFIED?

In the decades since the Korean War ended, more than a thousand South Korean soldiers have been killed in military skirmishes along the border between the two nations, which remained an ugly no-man's-land bristling with armed men, heavy weapons (tanks and artillery), and barbed wire. But during the last few years of the twentieth century, South Korean president Kim Dae Jung began reaching out diplomatically to North Korea in an attempt to reunify the two countries. And North Korea's growing economic problems led Premier Kim Jong Il to end his nation's international isolation and begin listening to the South Korean overtures.

After preliminary negotiations over several years, the two Kims—Kim is a common last name in Korea, and the leaders are not related—met in Pyongyang on June 13–15, 2000, on the eve of the fiftieth anniversary of the start of the Korean War. When the historic talks were over, Kim Dae Jung pronounced them a great success: "The Korean people can see a bright future as a dawn of hope for reconciliation, cooperation and unification is breaking."[156] On October 13, 2000, Kim won the Nobel Peace Prize for his efforts over several decades to reunite the two Koreas.

The immediate benefits of the new agreements the two leaders made were $450 million in new South Korean economic aid to North Korea, a reopening of the borders, re-connection of railroad lines, and more normal relations. The emotional reunions in August of Korean family members who had not seen one another in a half century were the most visible and poignant examples of the friendlier new relationship, but reunification, a dream shared by millions of North and South Koreans, will be a long, difficult process. In an article on the summit in *Maclean's* magazine, Tom Fennell and Susah Oh wrote:

> Dragging North Korea's 21 million people into the 21st century will ultimately require the North to merge with the South—a process that could take decades and cost $800 billion. . . . Despite the high price, polls show most of South Korea's 46 million people want to unite. "It's not a matter of cost," says Kim Hyun Ho [one of 10 million South Koreans with relatives in the North], "but of national pride."[157]

A FORGOTTEN WAR?

In the United States, the fiftieth anniversary of the Korean War sparked remembrances of and a new appreciation for the sacrifices American soldiers made in what is sometimes referred to as the "Forgotten War." On June 25, 2000, President Bill Clinton proclaimed:

> We have not forgotten. We pay honor to the courage of our veterans who fought in Korea and to the thousands who died there or whose fate is still unknown. We recall the grief of their families and the gratitude of the people of

South Korea. We remember that, in the Korean War, our soldiers' brave stand against Communism laid the foundations of peace and freedom that so many nations enjoy today.[158]

Clinton's comments echoed sentiments first voiced by President Truman, who in a July 4 , 1951, address said:

> Some things have not changed at all since 1776. For one thing, freedom is still expensive. It still costs money. It still costs blood. It still calls for courage and endurance, not only in soldiers, but in every man and woman who is free and who is determined to remain free.[159]

AN OLYMPIC MOMENT

For Koreans, however, the war is not history to be remembered, but something that affects their lives even today by dividing their ancient land; the war will never be over for them until North and South Korea are once again united. A glimpse of how wonderful this could be—when, and if, it ever happens—was seen on September 15, 2000, when athletes from both Koreas marched together at the opening ceremonies of the Summer Olympics in Sydney, Australia.

The procession of athletes who once considered each other enemies, many of them holding hands, brought the crowd of 110,000 to its feet. Chung Eun-sun, a star basketball player from South Korea, said,

Athletes from North and South Korea march together under one flag at the opening ceremonies of the 2000 Summer Olympics.

"It was a good show of unity to the world," while Yun Sung Bom of North Korea admitted, "I was deeply moved. I hope this mood will continue."[160] If the triumphal Olympic march was a sign of the future, then the Korean War may one day finally be over for North and South Koreans alike.

Notes

Introduction: The War Without a Winner

1. Quoted in Joseph C. Goulden, *Korea: The Untold Story of the War*. New York: McGraw-Hill Book Company, 1982, p. 4.

2. Quoted in Goulden, *Korea*, p. 3.

3. John Toland, *In Mortal Combat: Korea, 1950–1953*. New York: William Morrow and Company, Inc., 1991, p. 595.

4. Toland, *In Mortal Combat*, p. 7.

5. Jon Halliday and Bruce Cumings, *Korea: The Unknown War*. New York: Pantheon Books, 1988, p. 10.

6. Quoted in David McCullough, *Truman*. New York: Simon & Schuster, 1992, p. 777.

7. Quoted in Charles Patterson, *The Oxford 50th Anniversary Book of the United Nations*. New York: Oxford University Press, 1995, p. 40.

Chapter 1: The Cold War Begins

8. Quoted in Harold Evans, *The American Century*. New York: Alfred A. Knopf, 1998, p. 391.

9. Quoted in Bernard Baruch, *Baruch: The Public Years*. New York: Holt, Rinehart and Winston, 1960, p. 389.

10. Robert Kelley, *The Shaping of the American Past: Vol. 2, 1865 to Present*, fifth edition. Englewood Cliffs, NJ: Prentice-Hall, 1977, p. 672.

11. Robert Leckie, *The Wars of America*. New York: Harper & Row, Publishers, 1968, p. 835.

12. Quoted in the Editors of Time-Life Books. *The American Dream: The 50s*. Alexandria, VA: Time-Life Books, 1997, p. 20.

13. Quoted in Martin Walker, *The Cold War: A History*. New York: Henry Holt and Company, 1993, p. 14.

14. Quoted in Evans, *The American Century*, p. 318.

15. Quoted in Paul Johnson, *A History of the American People*. New York: HarperCollins, Publishers, 1997, p. 789.

16. Quoted in Johnson, *A History of the American People*, p. 790.

17. Leckie, *The Wars of America*, p. 819.

18. Quoted in McCullough, *Truman*, p. 372.

19. Quoted in Walker, *The Cold War*, p. 17.

20. Quoted in Robert L. Polley, ed., *The Truman Years: The Words and Times of Harry S. Truman*. Waukesha, WI: Country Beautiful, 1986, p. 10.

21. Quoted in Polley, ed., *The Truman Years*, p. 1.

22. Allan Nevins and Henry Steele Commager, *A Pocket History of the United States*, ninth revised edition. New York: Pocket Books, 1992, p. 469.

23. Quoted in Polley, ed., *The Truman Years*, p. 48.

24. Quoted in Johnson, *A History of the American People*, p. 804.

25. Quoted in Johnson, *A History of the American People*, p. 805.

26. Quoted in Johnson, *A History of the American People*, p. 805.

27. Quoted in McCullough, *Truman*, p. 445.

28. Kelley, *The Shaping of the American Past*, p. 665.

Chapter 2: The Cold War Turns Hot in Korea

29. Quoted in Goulden, *Korea*, p. 4.

30. Walker, *The Cold War*, p. 29.

31. Quoted in Goulden, *Korea*, p. 19.

32. Doug Dowd, "Cry 'Havoc!' and let slip the dogs of war: McCarthyism, Korea, and other nightmares." *Monthly Review*, April 1997, p. 32+.

33. Quoted in Johnson, *A History of the American People*, p. 807.

34. Quoted in Walker, *The Cold War*, p. 49.

35. Quoted in Leckie, *The Wars of America*, p. 841.

36. Quoted in Kelley, *The Shaping of the American Past: Vol. 2*, p. 676.

37. Quoted in Nevins and Commager, *A Pocket History of the United States*, p. 485.

38. Johnson, *A History of the American People*, p. 822.

39. Halliday and Cumings, *Korea: The Unknown War*, p. 10.

40. Halliday and Cumings, *Korea: The Unknown War*, p. 16.

41. Bruce Cumings, *Korea's Place in the Sun: A Modern History*. New York: W.W. Norton & Company, 1997, p. 149.

42. Quoted in Goulden, *Korea*, p. 15.

43. Dowd, "Cry 'Havoc!,'" *Monthly Review*, April 1997, p. 32+

44. Clay Blair, *The Forgotten War: America in Korea, 1950–1953*. New York: Anchor Books, Doubleday, 1987, p. 39.

45. Toland, *In Mortal Combat*, p. 17.

Chapter 3: North Korea Surprises the World

46. Quoted in Walker, *The Cold War*, p. 73.

47. Quoted in Evans, *The American Century*, p. 421.

48. Stanley Sandler, *The Korean War: No Victors, No Vanquished*. Lexington: The University Press of Kentucky, 1999, p. 43.

49. Quoted in Cumings, *Korea's Place in the Sun*, p. 253.

50. Quoted in Sandler, *The Korean War*, p. 41.

51. Sandler, *The Korean War*, p. 35.

52. Quoted in Johnson, *A History of the American People*, p. 824.

53. Quoted in Sandler, *The Korean War*, p. 30.

54. Quoted in Kelley, *The Shaping of the American Past*, p. 685.

55. Quoted in Leckie, *The Wars of America*, p. 851.

56. Quoted in Polley, ed., *The Truman Years*, p. 51.

57. Quoted in Gouldren, *Korea*, p. 88.

58. Quoted in Toland, *In Mortal Combat*, p. 53.

59. Quoted in Blair, *The Forgotten War*, p. 81.

60. Quoted in McCullough, *Truman*, p. 781.

61. Quoted in Goulden, *Korea*, p. 123.

62. Quoted in Goulden, *Korea*, p. 123.

63. Quoted in Leckie, *The Wars of America*, p. 866.

64. Stanley Weintraub, *MacArthur's War: Korea and the Undoing of an American Hero*. New York: The Free Press, 2000, p. 81.

65. Quoted in Weintraub, *MacArthur's War*, p. 81.

66. Quoted in Blair, *The Forgotten War*, p. 168.

Chapter 4: Victory at Inchon, Disaster When China Enters the War

67. Quoted in McCullough, *Truman*, p. 793.

68. Quoted in Weintraub, *MacArthur's War*, p. 118.

69. Quoted in Lawrence S. Wittner, ed., *MacArthur*. Englewood Cliffs, NJ: Prentice-Hall, Inc., 1971, p. 9.

70. Quoted in Kelley, *The Shaping of the American Past*, p. 658.

71. Quoted in Toland, *In Mortal Combat*, p. 179.

72. Quoted in Leckie, *The Wars of America*, p. 877.

73. Quoted in Sandler, *The Korean War*, p. 195.

74. Dolan, *America in the Korean War*, p. 45.

75. Quoted in Blair, *The Forgotten War*, p. 273.

76. Quoted in Goulden, *Korea*, p. 230.

77. Quoted from document at the United Nations internet site, www.un.org.

78. Quoted in Goulden, *Korea*, p. 237.

79. Quoted in Goulden, *Korea*, p. 239.

80. Quoted in Weintraub, *MacArthur's War*, p. 199.

81. Quoted in Toland, *In Mortal Combat*, p. 235.

82. Quoted in Weintraub, *MacArthur's War*, p. 176.

83. Quoted in Steven Hugh Lee, *Outposts of Empire: Korea, Vietnam, and the Origins of the Cold War in Asia, 1949–1954*. Montreal, Canada: McGill-Queen's University Press, 1996, p. 94.

84. Quoted in Weintraub, *MacArthur's War*, p. 185.

85. Quoted in Blair, *The Forgotten War*, p. 377.

86. Quoted in Leckie, *The Wars of America*, p. 889.

87. Quoted in McCullough, *Truman*, p. 815.

88. Toland, *In Mortal Combat*, p. 272.

89. Dolan, *America in the Korean War*, p. 427.

90. Leckie, *The Wars of America*, p. 899.

91. Quoted in Weintraub, *MacArthur's War*, p. 278.

Chapter 5: The Korean War Divides America

92. Quoted in Goulden, *Korea*, p. 85.

93. Quoted in Leckie, *The Wars of America*, p. 867.

94. Toland, *In Mortal Combat*, p. 71.

95. Quoted in Leckie, *The Wars of America*, p. 837.

96. Goulden, *Korea*, p. xvi.

97. Quoted in Goulden, *Korea*, p. 136.

98. Quoted in Maitland A. Edey, *This Fabulous Century: Volume VI, 1950–1960*. The Editors of Time-Life Books. New York, NY: Time-Life Books, 1970, p. 25.

99. Walker, *The Cold War*, p. 69.

100. Quoted in David Halberstam, *The Fifties*. New York: Villard Books, 1993, p. 10.

101. Quoted in McCullough, *Truman*, p. 814.

102. Quoted in McCullough, *Truman*, p. 817.

103. Quoted in Wittner, ed., *MacArthur*, p. 155.

104. Quoted in Goulden, *Korea*, p. 139.

105. Quoted in Wilson A. Heefner, "The Inch'on Landing." *Military Review*, March/April 1995, p. 65+.

106. Quoted in Weintraub, *MacArthur's War*, p. 249.

107. Quoted in Goulden, *Korea*, p. 481.

108. Quoted in McCullough, *Truman*, p. 838.

109. Quoted in Harry S. Truman, "Address on the Recall of General MacArthur." *The Department of State Bulletin*, April 16, 1951, pp. 603–05.

110. Quoted in Wittner, ed., *MacArthur*, p. 121.

111. Quoted in Halberstam, *The Fifties*, p. 115.

112. Quoted in Harold Stassen and Marshall Houts, *Eisenhower*. St. Paul, MN: Merrill/Magnus Publishing Corporation, 1990, p. 67.

113. Quoted in Edey, ed., *This Fabulous Century*, p. 38.

114. Quoted in McCullough, *Truman*, p. 854.

115. Quoted in Johnson, *A History of the American People*, p. 831.

116. Quoted in Edey, ed., *This Fabulous Century*, p. 118.

117. Quoted in Halberstam, *The Fifties*, p. 52.

118. Quoted in Kelley, *The Shaping of the American Past*, p. 706.

119. Quoted in Polley, ed., *The Truman Years*, p. 109.

120. Quoted in McCullough, *Truman*, p. 831.

Chapter 6: Waging Peace to End a War

121. Quoted in Goulden, *Korea*, p. 552.

122. Quoted in Goulden, *Korea*, p. 434.

123. Quoted in Toland, *In Mortal Combat*, p. 395.

124. Sandler, *The Korean War*, p. 240.

125. Quoted in Sandler, *The Korean War*, p. 247.

126. Halliday and Cumings, *Korea: The Unknown War*, p. 90.

127. Quoted in McCullough, *Truman*, p. 788.

128. Quoted in McCullough, *Truman*, p. 796.

129. Quoted in Stella Kim, "The Bridge at No Gun Ri." *Time*, October 11, 1999, p. 42.

130. Quoted in Halliday and Cumings, *Korea: The Unknown War*, p. 88.

131. Toland, *In Mortal Combat*, p. 152.

132. Quoted in Goulden, *Korea*, p. 296.

133. Sandler, *The Korean War*, p. 61.

134. Halliday and Cumings, *Korea: The Unknown War*, p. 178.

135. Quoted in Goulden, *Korea*, p. xxxv.

136. Quoted in Leckie, *The Wars of America*, p. 917.

137. Quoted in McCullough, *Truman*, p. 912.

138. Quoted in Stassen and Houts, *Eisenhower*, p. 81.

139. Quoted in Toland, *In Mortal Combat*, p. 557.

140. Quoted in Goulden, *Korea*, p. 646.

141. Quoted in Goulden, *Korea*, p. 645.

Chapter 7: Aftermath: The War with No Peace

142. Quoted in Stephanie Strom, "100 Korean families reunited in Seoul." *New York Times*, August 16, 2000, p. 3A.

143. Quoted in Lindesay Parrott, "Truce Is Signed, Ending Fighting in Korea." *New York Times*, July 27, 1953, p. 1.

144. Goulden, *Korea*, p. xv.

145. Halliday and Cumings, *Korea: The Unknown War*, p. 202.

146. Quoted in Evans, *The American Century*, p. 402.

147. Quoted in Goulden, *Korea*, p. xv.

148. David Rees, consultant editor, *The Korean War: History and Tactics*. New York: Crescent Books, 1984, p. 124.

149. Halliday and Cumings, *Korea*, p. 202.

150. Walker, *The Cold War*, p. 78.

151. Quoted in Walker, *The Cold War*, p. 66.

152. Quoted in Halliday and Cumings, *Korea: The Unknown War*, p. 152.

153. Lee, *Outposts of Empire*, p. 189.

154. Paul Shin, "Two Koreas find they're worlds apart in spirit." Associated Press, June 11, 2000.

155. Quoted in David E. Sanger, "Kim Il Sung Dead at Age 82; Led North Korea for 5 Decades." *New York Times*, July 9, 1994, p. 1.

156. Tom Fennell and Susah Oh, "Two Kims bridge Korea's two solitudes." *Maclean's*, June 26, 2000, p. 35.

157. Fennell and Oh, "Two Kims," p. 35.

158. Quoted in "Clinton Statement on War Anniversary." Associated Press, June 24, 2000.

159. Quoted in Polley, ed., *The Truman Years*, p. 88.

160. Shin, "Two Koreas."

For Further Reading

Edward F. Dolan, *America in the Korean War*. Brookfield, CT: The Millbrook Press, 1998. An authoritative explanation of the war with many pictures that illustrate and complement the text.

Maitland A. Edey, ed., *This Fabulous Century: Volume 6, 1950–1960*. The Editors of Time-Life Books. New York, NY: Time-Life Books, 1970. An interesting, easy to read portrayal of the 1950s that captures the way people lived and their reactions to major events.

Harold Evans, *The American Century*. New York, NY: Alfred A. Knopf, 1998. A well-written, easy to read history of the twentieth century.

Jon Halliday and Bruce Cumings, *Korea: The Unknown War*. New York: Pantheon Books, 1988. These knowledgeable military writers vividly explain how the war was fought and what soldiers had to endure in battle.

Jeremy Isaacs and Taylor Downing, *Cold War: An Illustrated History, 1945–1991*. New York: Little, Brown and Company. 1998. An excellent, very readable history of the Cold War, with interesting pictures that capture the feel of the period.

William Leuchtenburg and the Editors of Time-Life Books, *The Time-Life History of the United States, Volume 12: From 1945*. New York: Time-Life Books, 1974. An easy to read look at the history of the United States from the end of World War II through the Vietnam War.

Charles Patterson, *The Oxford 50th Anniversary Book of the United Nations*. New York: Oxford University Press, 1995. This book examines how the United Nations was formed and its involvement in world events in its first half century.

John Toland, *In Mortal Combat: Korea, 1950–1953*. New York: William Morrow and Company, Inc., 1991. Perhaps the best book ever written on the war, by an author who won the Pulitzer Prize for his work on Japan.

Works Consulted

Books

Bernard Baruch, *Baruch: The Public Years*. New York: Holt, Rinehart and Winston, 1960. The second volume of Baruch's autobiography focuses on his public life, including his years as a United Nations diplomat.

Clay Blair, *The Forgotten War: America in Korea, 1950–1953*. New York: Anchor Books, Doubleday, 1987. A detailed study of the first year of the war by a former journalist who has written extensively about America's twentieth-century wars.

Bruce Cumings, *Korea's Place in the Sun: A Modern History*. New York: W.W. Norton & Company, 1997. A scholarly, highly academic look at Korea's long history.

D. Duane Cummins, William Gee White. *Combat and Consensus: The 1940's and 1950's*. Encino, CA: Glencoe Publishing Co., Inc., 1972. An interesting look at how the American public has supported and opposed U.S. involvement in various wars.

Joseph C. Goulden, *Korea: The Untold Story of the War*. New York: McGraw-Hill Book Company, 1982. One of the best and most comprehensive histories of the war and how Americans reacted to it.

David Halberstam, *The Fifties*. New York: Villard Books, 1993. The author examines the historical events and socio-economic trends that changed America in this decade.

Arthur Herman, *Joseph McCarthy: Reexamining the Life and Legacy of America's Most Hated Senator*. New York: The Free Press, 2000. A scholarly but very readable account of the career of this Wisconsin senator, who played a big part in the Red Scare of the 1950s.

Paul Johnson, *A History of the American People*. New York: HarperCollins, Publishers, 1997. A readable, informative book that details the major events in America's history and explains why they happened.

Robert Kelley, *The Shaping of the American Past: Vol. 2, 1865 to Present*. Fifth edition. Englewood Cliffs, NJ: Prentice-Hall, 1977. A solid overall history of how the United States grew and changed over the decades from 1865.

George F. Kennan, *At a Century's Ending: Reflections, 1982–1995*. New York: W.W. Norton & Company, 1996. The architect of America's containment policy reflects on the Cold War and other issues in this collection of essays, reviews, and speeches.

Robert Leckie, *The Wars of America*. New York: Harper & Row, Publishers, 1968. This World War II Marine explains the nation's participation in all of its wars.

Steven Hugh Lee, *Outposts of Empire: Korea, Vietnam, and the Origins of the Cold War in Asia, 1949–1954.* Montreal, Canada: McGill-Queen's University Press, 1996. A scholarly but rather dry work on how the United States, Great Britain, and Canada formed their Cold War policy.

David McCullough, *Truman.* New York: Simon & Schuster, 1992. A very good biography of Harry S. Truman.

Allan Nevins and Henry Steele Commager, *A Pocket History of the United States.* New York: Pocket Books, 1992, ninth revised edition. A concise, condensed review of American history that not only lists the major events that shaped America but explains their importance.

Robert L. Polley, ed., *The Truman Years: The Words and Times of Harry S. Truman.* Waukesha, WI: Country Beautiful, 1986. A collection of quotations and writings by Truman on a wide variety of subjects, from his private life to his decision to drop the atomic bomb on Hiroshima.

David Rees, consultant editor, *The Korean War: History and Tactics.* New York: Crescent Books, 1984. This noted military writer provides valuable background on the history underlying the conflict and explains how the war was fought.

Stanley Sandler, *The Korean War: No Victors, No Vanquished.* Lexington: The University Press of Kentucky, 1999. A vivid, informative, detailed history of the war that explains the divisions the conflict caused at home.

Harold Stassen and Marshall Houts, *Eisenhower.* St. Paul, MN: Merrill/Magnus Publishing Corporation, 1990. A weak biography of Eisenhower that nonetheless has some interesting background on his 1952 presidential campaign, in which Stassen worked.

Martin Walker, *The Cold War: A History.* New York: Henry Holt and Company, 1993. A detailed, interesting history of how the United States and Soviet Union waged this odd war for nearly five decades.

Stanley Weintraub, *MacArthur's War: Korea and the Undoing of an American Hero.* New York: The Free Press, 2000. The author takes a highly critical look at MacArthur and how his egotistical personality often led him into making bad military decisions.

Lawrence S. Wittner, ed., *MacArthur.* Englewood Cliffs, NJ: Prentice-Hall, Inc., 1971. A collection of quotes, speeches, and writings by MacArthur.

Magazines

Carl Bernard, "A Survivor's Guilt." *Newsweek,* March 8, 1999, p. 57.

Doug Dowd, "Cry 'Havoc!' and let slip the dogs of war: McCarthyism, Korea, and other nightmares." *Monthly Review,* April 1997, p. 32+.

Tom Fennell and Susah Oh, "Two Kims bridge Korea's two solitudes." *Maclean's,* June 26, 2000, p. 35.

Wilson A. Heefner, "The Inch'on Landing." *Military Review,* March/April 1995, p. 65+.

Bob Hope and Pete Martin, "A century of Hope." *Saturday Evening Post*, July–August 1998, p. 30+.

Stella Kim, "The Bridge at No Gun Ri. *Time*, October 11, 1999, p. 42.

Mark Thompson, "The Military: Reports of Their Deaths Were Greatly Exaggerated," *Time*, June 12, 2000, p. 22.

Harry S. Truman, "Address on the Recall of General MacArthur." *The Department of State Bulletin*, April 16, 1951, pp. 603–05.

Newspapers

Lindesay Parrott, "Truce is Signed, Ending Fighting In Korea." *New York Times*, July 27, 1953, p. 1.

David E. Sanger, "Kim Il Sung Dead at Age 82; Led North Korea for 5 Decades." *New York Times*, July 9, 1994, p. 1.

Paul Shin, "Korean Athletes March Together." Associated Press, September 15, 2000.

Paul Shin, "Two Koreas find they're worlds apart in spirit." Associated Press, June 11, 2000.

Stephanie Strom, "100 Korean families reunited in Seoul." *New York Times*, August 16, 2000, p. 3A.

"Clinton Statement on War Anniversary." Associated Press, June 24, 2000.

Index

Picture Credits

About the Author

Michael V. Uschan has written thirteen books including *America's Founders*, a multiple biography of George Washington, Thomas Jefferson, and other early U.S. leaders, and biographies of President John F. Kennedy and Minnesota governor Jesse Ventura, all for Lucent Books. Mr. Uschan began his career as a writer and editor with United Press International, a wire service that provided stories to newspapers, radio, and television. Journalism is sometimes called "history in a hurry," and Mr. Uschan considers writing history books a natural extension of skills he developed in his many years as a working journalist. He and his wife, Barbara, reside in the Milwaukee suburb of Franklin, Wisconsin.